MEGAN KREINER

CLASSIC

Disney

CROCHET ®

12 PROJECTS FEATURING TIMELESS DISNEY CHARACTERS

Thunder Bay
P · R · E · S · S
SAN DIEGO, CALIFORN

Thunder Bay Press
An imprint of Printers Row Publishing Group
A division of Readerlink Distribution Services, LLC
10350 Barnes Canyon Road, Suite 100, San Diego, CA 92121
www.thunderbaybooks.com

Printers Row Publishing Group is a division of Readerlink Distribution Services, LLC.
The Thunder Bay Press name and logo are trademarks of Readerlink Distribution
Services, LLC.

All notations of errors or omissions should be addressed to Thunder Bay Press,
Editorial Department, at the above address. All other correspondence (author
inquiries, permissions) concerning the content of this book should be addressed to
becker&mayer! Books, 11120 NE 33rd Place, Ste. 101, Bellevue, WA 98004.

This book is part of the *Disney Classic Crochet* kit and is not to be sold
separately.

Produced by becker&mayer! LLC
Bellevue, Washington
www.beckermayer.com

Designer: Rosebud Eustace
Editor: Nicole Burns Ascue
Photographer: Joseph Lambert
Production coordinator: Jennifer Marx
Product development: Peter Schumacher

Project # 16184

Design elements used throughout, via Shutterstock unless otherwise noted:

Starry sky background © LilKar; Night sky background © Flame of Life;
Blue light bust © trucic.

ISBN: 978-1-62686-325-5

Printed, manufactured, and assembled in Shenzhen, China.

20 19 18 17 16   4 5 6 7 8

CONTENTS

INTRODUCTION

I am a big fan of all things Disney. I love the movies, the characters, and visiting Disney parks whenever I can. I love animation so much that I became an animator after graduating from college—while designing crochet patterns in my spare time, of course.

Now you can create a little Disney magic of your own with just a crochet hook, a few skeins of yarn, and this book. Inside you'll find a dozen classic Disney character projects complete with carefully crafted details like Minnie Mouse's pillbox hat, Jiminy Cricket's handy umbrella, and Donald Duck's darling bowtie.

I hope you'll have as much fun making these timeless characters as I had designing them.

Happy crocheting!

—Megan Kreiner of MK Crochet

WHAT'S INCLUDED

This kit contains the materials you will need to make one Mickey Mouse and one Donald Duck. Included are the following: a size G/6 (4 mm) crochet hook; a metal tapestry needle; yarn in colors white, black, blue, yellow, and red; felt in black, light blue, and white; thread in black and white; and fiberfill.

TerMINOLOGY ANd TecHNIQUES

SLIP KNOT

This is the basic knot used at the beginning of a chain and as a base for the adjustable ring.

1. Make a loop with a 6" tail. Overlap the loop on top of the yarn coming out of the skein. (Fig. A)

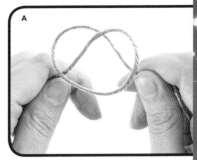

2. Slip your hook into the loop and under the working yarn. Pull to tighten the yarn around the hook. (Fig. B)

CHAIN (CH) AND YARN OVER (YO)

1. Begin by making a slip knot on your hook.

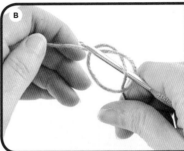

2. Yarn over (YO) by wrapping your yarn over the hook from back to front. Draw the yarn through the loop on your hook. You should now have 1 loop on your hook and the slip knot below it. (Fig. C)

3. Repeat step 2 until you've reached the specified number of chain stitches. When checking your work, only the chains below the loop on the hook should be counted. (Fig. D)

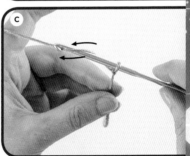

SLIP STITCH (SL ST)

Working as loosely as possible, insert your hook into the next chain or stitch. YO and draw the yarn through the loops on your hook. (Fig. E–page 6)

SINGLE CROCHET (SC)

1. Insert your hook into the next chain or stitch and YO. Draw the yarn through the chain or stitch. You will have 2 loops on your hook. (Fig. F–page 6)

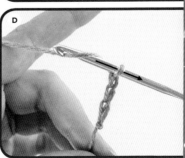

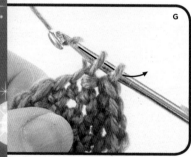

2. YO and draw yarn through both loops on your hook to finish the stitch. (Fig. G)

HALF DOUBLE CROCHET (HDC)

1. YO the hook and insert your hook into the next chain or stitch. YO a second time and draw the yarn through the chain or stitch. You will have 3 loops on your hook. (Fig. H)

2. YO and draw yarn through all 3 loops on your hook to finish the stitch. (Fig. I–page 7)

DOUBLE CROCHET (DC)

1. YO the hook and insert your hook into the next chain or stitch. YO a second time and draw the yarn through the chain or stitch. You will have 3 loops on your hook. (Fig. J)

2. YO and draw yarn through the first 2 loops on your hook. You will have 2 loops remaining on your hook. (Fig. K)

3. YO and draw yarn through the remaining 2 loops on your hook to finish the stitch. (Fig. L)

TRIPLE CROCHET (TR)

1. YO the hook 2 times and insert your hook into the next chain or stitch. YO a third time and draw the yarn through the chain or stitch. You will have 4 loops on your hook.

2. YO and draw yarn through the first 2 loops on your hook. You will have 3 loops remaining on your hook. (Fig. M–page 8)

3. YO and draw yarn through the next 2 loops on your hook. You will have 2 loops remaining on your hook. (Fig. N–page 8)

4. YO and draw yarn through the remaining 2 loops on your hook to finish the stitch. (Fig. O–page 8)

INCREASES (SC 2 IN NEXT ST)

The most common increase in this book, simply work 2 or more stitches into the same stitch. (Fig. P–page 8)

DECREASES

You will find two kinds of decreases within this book: single crochet decreases and skipped stitches.

SINGLE CROCHET 2 TOGETHER (SC2TOG)

1. Insert your hook into the next stitch. YO and draw the yarn through the stitch. You will have 2 loops on your hook.

2. Repeat step 1 in the following stitch. You will have 3 loops on your hook.

3. YO and draw yarn through all 3 loops on your hook to finish the decrease. (Fig. Q–page 9)

SKIP (SK)

Per the pattern instructions, count and skip the number of stitches indicated before proceeding with the next stitch.

PLACE MARKER (PM)

Markers can be used to help you locate a specific spot on your piece, such as the start and end of a round, the corners of a square shape, or a point for an assembly step. A marker can be as simple as a tied-on piece of scrap yarn or a safety pin. Split or locking rings also work well.

When a pattern calls for a place marker, place the marker in the last stitch you made and leave it in place as you continue to crochet unless you are instructed to move the marker to the next round. Stitch markers used to mark the beginnings or ends of rounds are automatically moved up.

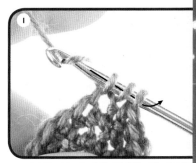

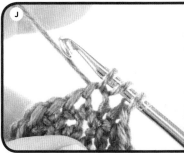

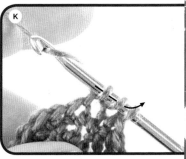

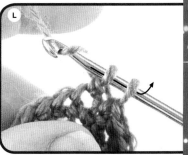

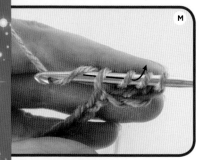

WORKING IN BACK LOOPS (BLO), FRONT LOOPS (FLO), AND BOTH LOOPS (TBL)

Unless otherwise indicated, work in both loops of a stitch except when the pattern instructs that a stitch should be worked in the back loop or front loop. The back loop will be the loop farthest from you, and the front loop is the loop closest to you.

If a pattern says, *In flo; sc 3, tbl; sc 5, in blo; sc 2. (10 sts),* you would single crochet 3 in the front loops, single crochet 5 in both loops, and single crochet 2 in the back loops for 10 stitches total. (Fig. R)

RIGHT SIDE (RS) VS. WRONG SIDE (WS)

When working in the round, you will want to keep track of which side of the pattern is the right side. It will affect which part of the stitch you'll perceive as the back loop versus the front loop. Generally, the 6″ tail left over from forming the adjustable ring will lie on the wrong side of the piece. The same can be said for patterns started by working around a chain when the tail is kept at the back of your work during the first round.

ADJUSTABLE RING

Use the adjustable ring technique to hide the hole that commonly appears in the middle of the starting round.

1. Form a ring with your yarn, leaving a 6″ tail. Insert the hook into the loop as if you were making a slip knot. (Fig. S)

2. YO the hook and pull through the loop to make a slip stitch. (Fig. T)

3. Chain 1 and then single crochet over both strands of yarn that make up the edge of the adjustable ring until you reach the number of stitches indicated in the pattern. To close the center of the ring, pull firmly on the yarn tail. (Fig. U–page 10)

To start the next round, work your next stitch in the first single crochet of the completed adjustable ring. If the pattern calls for a semicircle shape, you'll be instructed to chain 1 and turn the work so that the back of the piece faces you before you continue working the next row in your pattern.

WORKING IN THE ROUND

Patterns in this book are worked in a continuous spiral in which you simply keep crocheting from one round to the next. To help you keep track of where your row begins and ends, use a split or locking ring to mark either the first or last stitch of your round.

WORKING AROUND A CHAIN

A few patterns in this book begin by working around a chain of stitches. After creating your chain, you'll first work in the back ridge loops of the chain and then in the front loops of the chain. (Fig. V–page 10)

1. Make a chain per the pattern instructions. Starting in the second chain from the hook, work your first stitch in the back ridge loops of the chain and mark it with a split or locking ring. Continue working down the chain into the back ridge loops until you reach the last chain next to the slip knot. Work the indicated number of stitches into the back ridge loop of this last chain. (Fig. W–page 10)

2. When you're ready to begin the other side of the chain, rotate your work so the front loops of the chain are facing up. Starting in the second chain

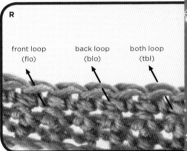

front loop (flo)   back loop (blo)   both loop (tbl)

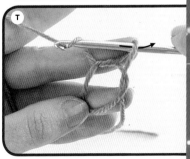

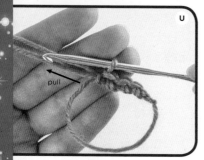

from the slip knot, insert your hook under the 2 front loops of the chain to work your next stitch. (Fig. X)

3. Once you have finished working the rest of the stitches into the front loops of round 1, continue on to round 2 and work your next stitch into the marked first stitch of round 1. (Fig. Y)

WORKING IN ROWS

For pattern pieces that are worked in rows, there will be a "turning" chain at the end of the finished row, which will be skipped over when you are ready to begin the next row.

WORKING IN A CHAIN SPACE (CH SP)

Proceed with making your next stitch as you normally would, but in this instance, work your stitches into the space below the chain.

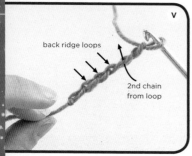

CHANGING COLORS

Work the stitch prior to the color change up to the last step in which you would draw the yarn through the loop(s) on your hook to complete the stitch. To change colors, YO the hook with your new color and draw the new color through the remaining loop(s) on your hook to complete the stitch. You can then continue on to the next stitch in the new color.

For color changes at the beginning of a new row, complete the stitch in your previous row, and then introduce the new color as you chain 1 and turn. Continue to work with your new color for the next row. (Fig. Z)

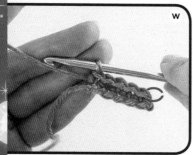

For color changes that take place in a slip stitch, simply insert the hook into the old color stitch, YO with the new color, and draw the new color through the loop on your hook to complete your slip stitch and the color change.

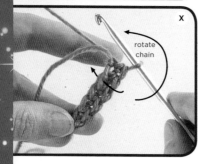

FINISHING TOUCHES

LONG STITCH

Use this stitch to help shape the surface of your character. With your yarn and a metal tapestry needle, draw the yarn up through the surface of your piece and then reinsert the needle in a different location. Repeat if desired to double or triple up the yarn. To cinch the surface of your piece, pull the yarn firmly as you work. (Fig. Aa)

RUNNING STITCH

Use this stitch to attach felt pieces or flattened crochet pieces to your work. With thread and a sewing needle, draw your thread in and out of the surface of your piece in a dashed line pattern. (Fig. Bb)

BACK STITCH

Use this stitch to create line details on the surface of your piece. Begin by drawing the yarn up through the surface of your piece and then reinsert the needle at a second point. Next, draw your yarn up at a third point and then reinsert the needle at the second point. Continue to work in this manner to make a solid line of stitches. (Fig. Cc–page 12)

OVERCAST STITCH

Use this stitch to create long curved stitches on the face for eyebrows and mouth shapes. Begin by drawing the yarn up through the surface of your piece and then reinsert the needle at a second point, leaving the yarn loose to achieve the desired level of curve. Choose a point along the curved long stitch and draw up the yarn at a third point. Reinsert at a fourth point to hold the shape of the long stitch in

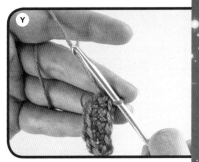

Cc

Dd

Ee

Ff

place. Feel free to repeat if desired at other points along the long stitch if needed. (Fig. Dd)

WHIP STITCH

Employ this stitch to close seams and attach open edges on your work. Using a tapestry needle and yarn, draw the needle and yarn through your work and catch the edge(s) of the second piece you wish to sew in place. Pull the yarn through the edge(s) before drawing the yarn through your work again in a spiral-like motion. Continue until the seam is closed or the piece is attached. (Fig. Ee)

ADDING HAIR

Insert your hook through a surface stitch on your work and fold a 4″ piece of yarn over the hook. Draw the yarn halfway through the surface stitch to create a small loop. Pull the loose ends of the yarn through this loop and pull tightly to secure it. For an even fuzzier look, use a steel tapestry needle to separate the yarn plys and trim as needed. (Fig. Ff)

TWISTED CORD

Use this technique to make a tail. Cut a length of yarn at least 4 to 6 times longer than your finished cord will be. Holding the cut ends in one hand, take the folded end in your other hand and hook your finger into the loop. Spin and rotate your finger to twist the yarn. Continue to twist until the yarn doubles over on itself. Measure out the final length of cord needed and tie the folded and cut ends together in a square knot to secure the twist. Sew the knotted end to the back of the body and work in the yarn ends. (Fig. Gg and Hh)

FELT PATCHES

The templates for the various patches used in this kit can be found on pages 86 and 87. You can use the templates with tracing paper, a photocopier, or a scanner.

If you prefer to glue your patches to your work instead of sewing with a needle and thread, consider picking up washable fabric glue.

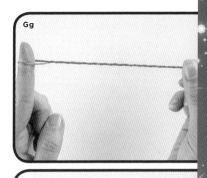

Gg

Hh

mickey mouse

Who's the leader of the club that's made for you and me? M-I-C-K-E-Y M-O-U-S-E! This classic Mickey Mouse is a must-have for any avid Disney fan. You can use the materials included in this kit to put your own Mickey Mouse together!

WHAT YOU'LL NEED

- G/6 (4mm) crochet hook
- Worsted weight yarn in black, yellow, red, and white
- Metal tapestry needle
- Black and white felt
- Fabric glue or needle and thread
- Stuffing

FINISHED SIZE: About 8" tall.

INSTRUCTIONS

HEAD

• In black, sc 8 in an adjustable ring.
Rnd 1: Sc 2 in each st around. (16 sts)
Rnd 2: *Sc 3, sc 2 in next st; rep from * 3 more times. (20 sts)
Rnd 3: *Sc 1, sc 2 in next st; rep from * 9 more times. (30 sts)
Rnd 4: *Sc 4, sc 2 in next st; rep from * 5 more times. (36 sts)
Rnds 5–9: Sc 36.
Rnd 10: *Sc 4, sc2tog; rep from * 5 more times. (30 sts)
Rnd 11: *Sc 1, sc2tog; rep from * 9 more times. (20 sts)
Rnd 12: *Sc 3, sc2tog; rep from * 3 more times. (16 sts)
• Stuff head.
Rnd 13: Sc2tog 8 times. (8 sts)
• Fasten off, leaving a long tail for sewing.

FACE

• In white, loosely ch 9.
Rnd 1: Starting in second chain from hook and working in back ridge loops, sc 7, sc 3 in next st. Rotate chain so front loops are facing up. Starting in next st and working in front loops, sc 6, sc 2 in next st. (18 sts)
Rnd 2: Sc 2 in next st, sc 1, hdc 1, dc 2, hdc 1, sc 1, sc 2 in next 3 sc, sc 2, hdc 2, sc 2, sc 2 in next 2 sts. (24 sts)
Rnd 3: Hdc 2 in next 2 sts, sc2tog, hdc 2, sc2tog, hdc 2 in next 2 sts, sc 4, sl st 6, sc 4. (26 sts)
• Place stitch pm in fifth st from hook. Cut and fasten off yarn. Rejoin yarn at pm and continue to work in rows.
Row 4: To rejoin white yarn, (sl st 1, ch 1, sc 3) in pm stitch, sc 3, sc 3 in next st, ch 1 and turn. Remove marker. (9 sts)
Row 5: Sk first chain, sc 2 in next st, sc

7, sc 2 in next st, ch 1 and turn. (11 sts)
Row 6: Sk first chain, sc 11, ch 1 and turn. (11 sts)
Row 7: Sk first chain, sc2tog, dc 3 in next st, sl st 1, sk 3, sl st 1, dc 3 in next st, sc2tog. (10 sts)
• Fasten off, leaving a long tail for sewing.

NOSE SHAPER

• In white, sc 6 in an adjustable ring.
Rnd 1: Sc 6.
Rnd 2: Sc 2 in each st around. (12 sts)
Rnds 3–4: Sc 12.
• Fasten off, leaving a long tail for sewing.

NOSE

• In black, sc 6 in an adjustable ring.
Rnd 1: Sc2tog 3 times. (3 sts)
• Fasten off, leaving a long tail for sewing.

EAR (MAKE 2)

• In black, sc 6 in an adjustable ring.
Rnd 1: Sc 2 in each st around. (12 sts)
Rnd 2: Sc 2 in each st around. (24 sts)
• Fasten off, leaving a long tail for sewing.

BODY

• In red, sc 10 in an adjustable ring.
Rnd 1: Sc 2 in each st around. (20 sts)
Rnd 2: Sc 20.
Rnd 3: *Sc 3, sc 2 in next st; rep from * 4 more times. (25 sts)
Rnds 4–5: Sc 25.
• Change to black.
Rnd 6: In blo; sc 25.
Rnd 7: *Sc 3, sc2tog; rep from * 4 more times. (20 sts)
Rnds 8–9: Sc 20.
Rnd 10: *Sc 3, sc2tog; rep from * 3 more times. (16 sts)
Rnd 11: Sc 16.
• Stuff body.
Rnd 12: Sc2tog 8 times. (8 sts)
• Fasten off, leaving a long tail for sewing.

HAND (MAKE 2)

• In white, sc 6 in an adjustable ring.
Rnd 1: Sc 2 in each st around. (12 sts)
Rnds 2–3: Sc 12.
Rnd 4: *Sc 1, sc2tog; rep from * 3 more times. (8 sts)
• Stuff hand.
Rnd 5: Sc2tog 4 times. (4 sts)
Rnd 6: In flo; sc 2 in each st around. (8 sts)
• Fasten off, leaving a long tail for sewing.

FINGER (MAKE 8)

• In white, sc 6 in an adjustable ring.
Rnd 1: Sc 6.
• Fasten off, leaving a long tail for sewing. Do not stuff.

ARM (MAKE 2)

• In black, sc 6 in an adjustable ring.
Rnds 1–4: Sc 6.
• Stuff arm. Flatten seam and sew closed, leaving a long tail for sewing.

LEG (MAKE 2)

• In black, sc 6 in an adjustable ring.

Rnds 1–2: Sc 6.
• Change to red.
Rnd 3: In flo; sc 2 in each st around. (12 sts)
Rnd 4: In blo; sc 12. (12 sts)
• Fasten off, leaving a long tail for sewing. Stuff leg.

SHOE (MAKE 2)

• In yellow, sc 8 in an adjustable ring.
Rnd 1: Sc 2 in each st around. (16 sts)
Rnd 2: Sc 16.
Rnd 3: *Sc 7, sc 2 in next st; rep from * 1 more time. (18 sts)
Rnd 4: *Sc 7, sc2tog; rep from * 1 more time. (16 sts)
Rnd 5: *Sc 2, sc2tog; rep from * 3 more times. (12 sts)
Rnds 6–8: Sc 12.
• Stuff shoe.
Rnd 9: Sc2tog 6 times. (6 sts)
• Fasten off and close hole. This is the back of the shoe. Sew in yarn ends.

SHOE TOP DETAIL

• In yellow, sc 8 in an adjustable ring.
Rnd 1: In blo; sl st 8.
• Fasten off, leaving a long tail for sewing.

TAIL

• In black, make a 3″ long twisted cord.

ASSEMBLY

1. Stuff and sew the open edge of the nose shaper to the lower half of the head. Lay the face over the nose shaper and sew in place. (Fig. A)

2. Once the face is sewn to the head, apply 2 to 3 long stitches across the bridge of the nose and pull tightly to shape the top of the nose bridge. (Fig. B)

3. Attach the open end of the nose to the face. Using black yarn, add a mouth. Cut out two eyes from the template using black felt, and glue or sew to the head. Sew the ears to the top of the head. (Fig. C)

4. Sew open ends of the fingers to the ends of the hands. Using black yarn, add 3 short stitches to the back of hands. (Figs. D, Dd)

5. Sew the open end of the head to the open end of the body. Using white yarn, sew the hands to the ends of the arms. Using the leftover yarn tail, sew the arms to the body at the shoulders. (Fig. E–page 18)

6. With the rounder end of the shoe at the front, attach the shoe top detail to the top of the shoe. Insert and sew the end of the leg into the shoe top detail. Attach the open end of the legs to the bottom portion of the body and close the seam. (Fig. F–page 18)

7. Cut out 4 buttons using white felt from template and glue or sew to the front and back of the pants.

8. Sew the 3″ tail cord to the back of the pants in between the white buttons. (Fig. G–page 18)

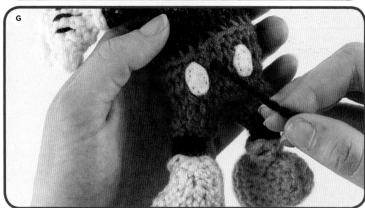

minnie
mouse

Who doesn't love Minnie Mouse? With a skirt covered in polka dots, chunky yellow pumps, and an adorable pillbox hat, she's ready for a fun time out with her best beau, Mickey Mouse!

WHAT YOU'LL NEED

- G/6 (4mm) crochet hook
- Worsted weight yarn in black, yellow, red, and white
- Metal tapestry needle
- Black and white felt
- Fabric glue or needle and thread
- Stuffing

FINISHED SIZE: About 7.5" tall.

INSTRUCTIONS

HEAD

• In black, sc 8 in an adjustable ring.

Rnd 1: Sc 2 in each st around. (16 sts)

Rnd 2: *Sc 3, sc 2 in next st; rep from * 3 more times. (20 sts)

Rnd 3: *Sc 1, sc 2 in next st; rep from * 9 more times. (30 sts)

Rnd 4: *Sc 4, sc 2 in next st; rep from * 5 more times. (36 sts)

Rnds 5–9: Sc 36.

Rnd 10: *Sc 4, sc2tog; rep from * 5 more times. (30 sts)

Rnd 11: *Sc 1, sc2tog; rep from * 9 more times. (20 sts)

Rnd 12: *Sc 3, sc2tog; rep from * 3 more times. (16 sts)

• Stuff head.

Rnd 13: Sc2tog 8 times. (8 sts)

• Fasten off, leaving a long tail for sewing.

FACE

• In white, loosely ch 9.

Rnd 1: Starting in second chain from hook and working in back ridge loops, sc 7, sc 3 in next st. Rotate chain so front loops are facing up. Starting in next st and working in front loops, sc 6, sc 2 in next st. (18 sts)

Rnd 2: Sc 2 in next st, sc 1, hdc 1, dc 2, hdc 1, sc 1, sc 2 in next 3 sc, sc 2, hdc 2, sc 2, sc 2 in next 2 sts. (24 sts)

Rnd 3: Hdc 2 in next 2 sts, sc2tog, hdc 2, sc2tog, hdc 2 in next 2 sts, sc 4, sl st 6, sc 4. (26 sts)

• Place stitch pm in 5th st from hook. Cut and fasten off yarn. After rejoining yarn at stitch marker, continue to work in rows.

Row 4: To rejoin white yarn; (sl st 1, ch 1, sc 3) in pm stitch, sc 3, sc 3 in next st, ch 1 and turn. Remove marker. (9 sts)

Row 5: Sk first chain, sc 2 in next st, sc 7, sc 2 in next st, ch 1 and turn. (11 sts)

Row 6: Sk first chain, sc 11, ch 1 and turn. (11 sts)

Row 7: Sk first chain, sc2tog, dc 3 in next st, sl st 1, sk 3, sl st 1, dc 3 in next st, sc2tog. (10 sts)

• Fasten off, leaving a long tail for sewing.

NOSE SHAPER

• In white, sc 6 in an adjustable ring.

Rnd 1: Sc 6.

Rnd 2: Sc 2 in each st around. (12 sts)

Rnds 3–4: Sc 12.

• Fasten off, leaving a long tail for sewing.

NOSE

• In black, sc 6 in an adjustable ring.

Rnd 1: Sc2tog 3 times. (3 sts)

• Fasten off, leaving a long tail for sewing.

EAR (MAKE 2)

• In black, sc 6 in an adjustable ring.

Rnd 1: Sc 2 in each st around. (12 sts)

Rnd 2: Sc 2 in each st around. (24 sts)

• Fasten off, leaving a long tail for sewing.

BODY

• In white, sc 10 in an adjustable ring.

Rnd 1: Sc 2 in each st around. (20 sts)

Rnd 2: Sc 20.

• Change to red.

Rnd 3: *Sc 3, sc 2 in next st; rep from * 4 more times. (25 sts)

Rnds 4–5: Sc 25.

• Change to black.

Rnd 6: In blo; sc 25.

Rnd 7: *Sc 3, sc2tog; rep from * 4 more times. (20 sts)

Rnds 8–9: Sc 20.

Rnd 10: *Sc 3, sc2tog; rep from * 3 more times. (16 sts)

Rnd 11: Sc 16.
- Stuff body.

Rnd 12: Sc2tog 8 times. (8 sts)
- Fasten off, leaving a long tail for sewing.

SKIRT

- In red, loosely ch 21 and turn.

Row 1: Starting in third chain from hook, 3 hdc in each st across. (60 sts)
- Fasten off, leaving a long tail for sewing.

TIP: *You can increase or decrease the number of chains if you would like a bigger or smaller skirt.*

HAND (MAKE 2)

- In white, sc 6 in an adjustable ring.

Rnd 1: Sc 2 in each st around. (12 sts)

Rnds 2-3: Sc 12.

Rnd 4: *Sc 1, sc2tog; rep from * 3 more times. (8 sts)
- Stuff hand.

Rnd 5: Sc2tog 4 times. (4 sts)

Rnd 6: In flo; sc 2 in each st around. (8 sts)
- Fasten off, leaving a long tail for sewing.

FINGER AND SHOE HEEL (MAKE 8 WHITE; MAKE 2 YELLOW)

- Sc 6 in an adjustable ring.

Rnd 1: Sc 6.
- Fasten off, leaving a long tail for sewing. Do not stuff.

ARM (MAKE 2)

- In black, sc 6 in an adjustable ring.

Rnds 1-4: Sc 6.
- Stuff arm. Flatten seam and sew closed, leaving a long tail for attachment.

LEG (MAKE 2)

- In black, sc 6 in an adjustable ring.

Rnd 1: In blo; sc 6.

Rnds 2-3: Sc 6.

- Change to white.

Rnd 4: In flo; (sl st 1, ch 3, sl st in sc at base of ch-3) in each st around. (6 ch-3 lps)
- Fasten off, leaving a long tail for sewing. Stuff leg lightly.

FOOT TOP (MAKE 2)

- In black, sc 6 in an adjustable ring.
- Fasten off, but do not join first and last stitches of the ring in order to retain a semicircle shape.

SHOE (MAKE 2)

- In yellow, sc 8 in an adjustable ring.

Rnd 1: Sc 2 in each st around. (16 sts)

Rnd 2: Sc 16.

Rnd 3: *Sc 7, sc 2 in next st; rep from * 1 more time. (18 sts)

Rnd 4: *Sc 7, sc2tog; rep from * 1 more time. (16 sts)

Rnd 5: *Sc 2, sc2tog; rep from * 3 more times. (12 sts)

Rnds 6-8: Sc 12.
- Stuff.

Rnd 9: Sc2tog 6 times. (6 sts)
- Fasten off and close hole. This is the front of the shoe. Sew in yarn ends.

PILLBOX HAT

- In red, sc 4 in an adjustable ring.

Rnd 1: Sc 2 in each st around. (8 sts)

Rnds 2-3: Sc 8.

Rnd 4: In flo; *sc 1, sc 2 in next st; rep from * 3 more times. (12 sts)

Rnd 5: In blo; *sc 3, sc 2 in next st; rep from * 2 more times. (15 sts)

Rnd 6: In blo; sl st 15.
- Fasten off, leaving long tail for sewing.

PILLBOX HAT FLOWER

- In white, sc 6 in an adjustable ring.

Rnd 1: Change to yellow, *sl st in next

st, ch 3, sl st 1 in st at base of ch-3; rep from * 5 more times. (6 ch-3 lps)

• Fasten off, leaving a long tail for sewing.

TAIL

• In black, make a 3" long twisted cord.

ASSEMBLY

1. Stuff and sew the open edge of the nose shaper to the lower half of the head. Lay the face over the nose shaper and sew in place. (Fig. A)

2. Once the face is sewn to the head, apply 2 to 3 long stitches across the bridge of the nose and pull tightly to shape the top of the nose bridge. (Fig. B)

3. Attach the open end of the nose to the face. Using black yarn, add a mouth. Cut out two felt eyes using black felt from template and glue or sew to the head. Sew ears to the top of the head. (Fig. C)

4. Attach the flower to the front of the hat and attach the hat to the head. Using black yarn, apply 3 short stitches to the upper corners of the eyes for eyelashes. (Fig. D)

5. Sew the open ends of the fingers to the ends of the hands. Using black yarn, add 3 short stitches to the back of the hands.

6. Sew the open end of the head to the open end of the body. Using white yarn, sew the hands to the ends of the arms. Using the leftover yarn tail, sew the arms to the body at the shoulders. (Fig. E–page 24)

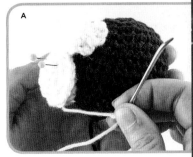

7. With the tapered end of the shoe at the front, sew the end of the leg onto the top of the shoe. Sew the foot top detail to the top of the shoe and the front edge of the leg. Sew the heel to the bottom of the shoe. (Fig. F)

8. Attach the open end of the legs to the white bottom portion of body. Wrap the skirt around the first red rnd of the body and secure with marking pins before sewing in place. (Fig. G)

9. Cut out about 10 felt spots using white felt from template and glue or sew around the red portion of the body. Sew the 3″ tail cord to the back of the body directly below the skirt line. (Fig. H)

DONALD DUCK

Donald Duck is my favorite Disney character. He might seem like a hothead, but I think it's only because he cares too much. You can use the materials in this kit to make your very own Donald Duck, complete with sailor shirt, cap, and charming demeanor!

WHAT YOU'LL NEED

- G/6 (4mm) crochet hook
- Worsted weight yarn in black, blue, yellow, red, and white
- Metal tapestry needle
- Black and light blue felt
- Fabric glue or needle and thread
- Stuffing

FINISHED SIZE: About 8" tall.

INSTRUCTIONS

HEAD

• In white, sc 8 in an adjustable ring.
Rnd 1: Sc 2 in each st around. (16 sts)
Rnd 2: *Sc 3, sc 2 in next st; rep from * 3 more times. (20 sts)
Rnd 3: *Sc 1, sc 2 in next st; rep from * 9 more times. (30 sts)
Rnd 4: *Sc 4, sc 2 in next st; rep from * 5 more times. (36 sts)
Rnds 5–8: Sc 36.
Rnd 9: *Sc 1, sc2tog; rep from * 11 more times. (24 sts)
Rnd 10: Sc 24.
Rnd 11: *Sc 1, sc2tog; rep from * 7 more times. (16 sts)
Rnd 12: Sc 16.
• Stuff head.
Rnd 13: Sc2tog 8 times. (8 sts)
• Fasten off, leaving a long tail for sewing.

TOP BEAK

• In yellow, loosely ch 8.
Rnd 1: Starting in second chain from hook and working in back ridge loops, sc 6, sc 3 in next st. Rotate chain so front loops are facing up. Starting in next st and working in front loops, sc 5, sc 2 in next st. (16 sts)
Rnds 2–3: Sc 16.
Rnd 4: *Sc 6, sc2tog; rep from * 1 more time. (14 sts)
Rnd 5: Sc 10, sc 2 in next st, (hdc 2, pm, hdc 1) in next st, sc 2 in next st, sc 1.
• Fasten off, leaving a long tail for sewing.
TIP: *Place marker indicates the top edge of the beak.*

BOTTOM BEAK

• In yellow, loosely ch 7.

Rnd 1: Starting in second chain from hook and working in back ridge loops, sc 5, sc 3 in next st. Rotate chain so front loops are facing up. Starting in next st and working in front loops, sc 4, sc 2 in next st. (14 sts)
Rnds 2–3: Sc 14.
Rnd 4: *Sc 5, sc2tog; rep from * 1 more time. (12 sts)
• Fasten off, leaving a long tail for sewing. Stuff lightly. Flatten seam and sew closed.

SIDE BEAK (MAKE 2)

• In yellow, sc 5 in an adjustable ring.
Rnds 1–6: Sc 5.
• Fasten off, leaving a long tail for sewing.

EYEBROW (MAKE 2)

• In white, loosely ch 6.
Row 1: Starting in second ch from hook, sc 5 in back ridge loops of chain.
• Fasten off, leaving a long tail for sewing.

HAT

• In blue, sc 6 in an adjustable ring.
Rnd 1: Sc 2 in each st around. (12 sts)
Rnd 2: Sc 3, hdc 2 in next 3 sts, sc 3, hdc 2 in next 3 sts. (18 sts)
Rnds 3–4: Sc 3, hdc 6, sc 3, hdc 6. (18 sts)
Rnd 5: Sc2tog 9 times. (9 sts)
• Change to black.
Rnd 6: In flo; sc 9. (9 sts)
Rnd 7: Sc 9.
• Fasten off, leaving a long tail for sewing. Stuff lightly.

BODY

• In white, sc 10 in an adjustable ring.
Rnd 1: Sc 2 in each st around. (20 sts)
Rnd 2: *Sc 1, sc 2 in next st; rep from * 9 more times. (30 sts)
Rnd 3: *Sc 2, sc 2 in next st; rep from * 9 more times. (40 sts)

Rnd 4: Sc 40.
Rnd 5: *Sc 2, sc2tog; rep from * 9 more times. (30 sts)
Rnd 6: *Sc 1, sc2tog; rep from * 9 more times. (20 sts)
• Change to blue.
Rnd 7: In flo; sc 20.
Rnds 8–9: Sc 20.
Rnd 10: *Sc 3, sc2tog; rep from * 3 more times. (16 sts)
Rnd 11: Sc 16.
• Stuff body.
Rnd 12: Sc2tog 8 times. (8 sts)
• Fasten off, leaving a long tail for sewing.

HAND AND ARM (MAKE 2)

• In white, sc 6 in an adjustable ring.
Rnd 1: Sc 2 in each st around. (12 sts)
Rnds 2–3: Sc 12.
Rnd 4: *Sc 1, sc2tog; rep from * 3 more times. (8 sts)
• Stuff hand.
Rnd 5: Sc2tog 4 times. (4 sts)
• Change to blue.
Rnd 6: In flo; sc 2 in each st around. (8 sts)
Rnds 7–8: Sc 8.
Rnd 9: *Sc 2, sc2tog; rep from * 1 more time. (6 sts)
• Stuff hand and arm. Flatten seam and sew closed, leaving a long tail for attachment.

FINGERS (MAKE 8)

• In white, sc 6 in an adjustable ring.
Rnd 1: Sc 6.
• Fasten off, leaving a long tail for sewing. Do not stuff.

BACK SHIRT PANEL

• In blue, loosely ch 7.
Row 1: Starting in second ch from hook, sc 6, ch 1 and turn. (6 sts)
Rows 2–3: Sk first ch, sc 6, ch 1 and turn. (6 sts)

- Fasten off, leaving a long tail for sewing.

BOW TIE
- In red, loosely ch 12 and join last chain to first chain with a slip stitch to form a ring.

Rnds 1–3: Sc 12.
- Fasten off, leaving a long tail for sewing.

LEG (MAKE 2)
- In yellow, loosely ch 6 and join last chain to first chain with a slip stitch to form a ring.

Rnds 1–3: Sc 6.
- Fasten off, leaving a long tail for sewing.

FOOT (MAKE 2)
- In yellow, sc 6 in an adjustable ring.

Rnd 1: Sc 2 in each st around. (12 sts)

Rnds 2–4: Sc 12.

Rnd 5: *Sc 2, sc 2 in next st; rep from * 3 more times. (16 sts)

Rnd 6: *Sc 7, sc 2 in next st; rep from * 1 more time. (18 sts)

Rnds 7–8: Sc 18.

Rnd 9: *(Hdc 1, dc 1, hdc 1) in next st, sk 1, sl st 1; rep from * 5 more times.
- Fasten off, leaving a long tail for sewing. Lightly stuff foot. Line up top edges and bottom of the three toes and whip stitch the open edge closed.

TAIL
- In white, loosely ch 20 and join last chain to first chain with a slip stitch to form a ring.

Rnd 1: Sc 3, sl st 7, sc 3, hdc 7. (20 sts)

Rnd 2: Sc2tog 3 times, sl st 2, sc2tog 4 times, hdc 2, sc2tog 1 time. (12 sts)

Rnd 3: Sc2tog 6 times. (6 sts)

Rnd 4: In flo; *(sl st 1, ch 5, sl st in sc at base of ch-5) in next st, sk 1; rep from * 2 more times.

- Fasten off, leaving a long tail for sewing. Using leftover yarn tail, cinch the space in the middle of rnd 4 closed by applying a running stitch around rnd 3.

ASSEMBLY

1. Sew the sewn edge of the bottom beak to the bottom edge of the top beak. (Fig. A–page 28)

2. Fold and attach the ends of the beak sides to the top and bottom corners of the top and bottom beak. (Fig. B–page 28)

3. Stuff and attach the beak to the lower half of the head. To help give the beak a flat shape, sew a line of running stitches 1 row in from the front edge of the beak through the top and bottom beak pieces. (Fig. C–page 28)

4. Cut out 2 eyes from light blue felt and 2 pupils from black felt using template. Glue or sew the felt pieces together before gluing or sewing the eyes to the front of the head. Sew eyebrows above the eyes. Sew the open edge of the hat to the top of the head and close the seam. Draw long stitches of black yarn along the crease between the top and bottom beak pieces. (Fig. D–page 29)

5. Cut out one hat ribbon from black felt using template. Glue or sew it to the back of the hat. (Fig. E–page 29)

6. Sew the open ends of the fingers to the ends of the hands.

7. Flatten the bow tie piece and wrap the tail tightly around the center to shape the two sides of the bow tie and secure. (Fig. F–page 29)

8. Sew the open end of the head to the open end of the body. Sew the arms to the body at the shoulders. Using yellow yarn and a tapestry needle, add a backstitch detail along the inside of the cuff. Sew the bow tie to the front of the shirt. (Fig. G–page 29)

9. Attach back shirt panel at the back of the neck. Using yellow yarn and a tapestry needle, add a backstitch detail along the inside of the back shirt panel. (Fig. H–page 30)

10. Sew one open edge of the leg to the top of the foot. Stuff the leg before sewing the top of the leg to the body. (Fig. I–page 30)

11. Position the tail against the lower back of the body and rotate so the hdc stitches are at the bottom of the piece. Pin and sew the open edge of the tail to the body. Stuff before closing seam. (Fig. J–page 30)

DAISY DUCK

Daisy Duck is as sassy as she is sweet. Rocking an extra-large pink bow with matching shoes, you can bet she's a lot of fun when she's out and about with Donald Duck.

WHAT YOU'LL NEED

- G/6 (4mm) crochet hook
- Worsted weight yarn in white, yellow, lavender, pink, and black
- Metal tapestry needle
- Black, light blue, and purple felt
- Fabric glue or needle and thread
- Stuffing

FINISHED SIZE: About 7" tall.

INSTRUCTIONS

HEAD

• In white, sc 8 in an adjustable ring.

Rnd 1: Sc 2 in each st around. (16 sts)

Rnd 2: *Sc 3, sc 2 in next st; rep from * 3 more times. (20 sts)

Rnd 3: *Sc 1, sc 2 in next st; rep from * 9 more times. (30 sts)

Rnd 4: *Sc 4, sc 2 in next st; rep from * 5 more times. (36 sts)

Rnds 5–8: Sc 36.

Rnd 9: *Sc 1, sc2tog; rep from * 11 more times. (24 sts)

Rnd 10: Sc 24.

Rnd 11: *Sc 1, sc2tog; rep from * 7 more times. (16 sts)

Rnd 12: Sc 16.

• Stuff head.

Rnd 13: Sc2tog 8 times. (8 sts)

• Fasten off, leaving a long tail for sewing.

TOP BEAK

• In yellow, loosely ch 8.

Rnd 1: Starting in second chain from hook and working in back ridge loops, sc 6, sc 3 in next st. Rotate chain so front loops are facing up. Starting in next st and working in front loops, sc 5, sc 2 in next st. (16 sts)

Rnds 2–3: Sc 16.

Rnd 4: *Sc 6, sc2tog; rep from * 1 more time. (14 sts)

Rnd 5: Sc 10, sc 2 in next st, (hdc 2, pm, hdc 1) in next st, sc 2 in next st, sc 1.

• Fasten off, leaving a long tail for sewing.

TIP: *Place marker indicates the top edge of the beak.*

BOTTOM BEAK

• In yellow, loosely ch 7.

Rnd 1: Starting in second chain from hook and working in back ridge loops, sc 5, sc 3 in next st. Rotate chain so front loops are facing up. Starting in next st and working in front loops, sc 4, sc 2 in next st. (14 sts)

Rnds 2–3: Sc 14.

Rnd 4: *Sc 5, sc2tog; rep from * 1 more time. (12 sts)

• Fasten off, leaving a long tail for sewing. Stuff lightly. Flatten seam and sew closed.

SIDE BEAK (MAKE 2)

• In yellow, sc 5 in an adjustable ring.

Rnds 1–6: Sc 5.

• Fasten off, leaving a long tail for sewing.

EYEBROW (MAKE 2)

• In white, loosely ch 6.

Row 1: Starting in second ch from hook, sc 5 in back ridge loops of chain.

• Fasten off, leaving a long tail for sewing.

BODY

• In white, sc 10 in an adjustable ring.

Rnd 1: Sc 2 in each st around. (20 sts)

Rnd 2: *Sc 1, sc 2 in next st; rep from * 9 more times. (30 sts)

Rnd 3: *Sc 2, sc 2 in next st; rep from * 9 more times. (40 sts)

Rnd 4: Sc 40.

Rnd 5: *Sc 2, sc2tog; rep from * 9 more times. (30 sts)

Rnd 6: *Sc 1, sc2tog; rep from * 9 more times. (20 sts)

• Change to lavender.

Rnd 7: In flo; sc 20.

Rnds 8–9: Sc 20.

Rnd 10: *Sc 3, sc2tog; rep from * 3 more times. (16 sts)

Rnd 11: Sc 16.

• Stuff body.

Rnd 12: Sc2tog 8 times. (8 sts)

• Fasten off, leaving a long tail for sewing.

HAND AND ARM (MAKE 2)

- In white, sc 6 in an adjustable ring.

Rnd 1: Sc 2 in each st around. (12 sts)

Rnds 2–3: Sc 12.

Rnd 4: *Sc 1, sc2tog; rep from * 3 more times. (8 sts)

- Stuff hand.

Rnd 5: *Sc 2, sc2tog; rep from * 1 more time. (6 sts)

Rnd 6: *Sc 2, sc 2 in next st; rep from * 1 more time. (8 sts)

Rnd 7: Sc 8.

- Change to lavender.

Rnd 8: In flo; sc 2 in each st around. (16 sts)

Rnd 9: *Sc 2, sc2tog; rep from * 3 more times. (12 sts)

Rnd 10: Sc2tog 6 times. (6 sts)

- Stuff arm. Flatten seam and sew closed, leaving a long tail for sewing.

FINGER AND SHOE HEEL (MAKE 8 WHITE; MAKE 2 PINK)

- Sc 6 in an adjustable ring.

Rnd 1: Sc 6.

- Fasten off, leaving a long tail for sewing. Do not stuff.

BOW

- In pink, loosely ch 20 and join last chain to first chain with a slip stitch to form a ring.

Rnds 1–3: Sc 20.

Rnd 4: Sc2tog 10 times. (10 sts)

Rnd 5: Sc 2 in each st around. (20 sts)

Rnds 6–8: Sc 20.

- Fasten off, leaving a long tail for sewing.

CREST

- In white, loosely ch 9.

Row 1: Starting in second ch from hook, *(sl st, ch 4, sl st at base of ch-4), sl st 1; rep from * 3 more times. (4 ch-4 lps)

- Fasten off, leaving a long tail for sewing.

LEG (MAKE 2)

- In yellow, sc 6 in an adjustable ring.

Rnd 1: In blo; sc 6.

Rnds 2–3: Sc 6.

- Change to white.

Rnd 4: In flo; (sl st 1, ch 3, sl st in sc at base of ch) in each st around. (6 ch-3 lps)

- Fasten off, leaving a long tail for sewing. Stuff leg.

FOOT TOP (MAKE 2)

- In yellow, sc 6 in an adjustable ring.
- Fasten off, but do not join first and last stitches of the ring in order to retain a semicircle shape.

SHOE (MAKE 2)

- In pink, sc 8 in an adjustable ring.

Rnd 1: Sc 2 in each st around. (16 sts)

Rnd 2: Sc 16.

Rnd 3: *Sc 7, sc 2 in next st; rep from * 1 more time. (18 sts)

Rnd 4: *Sc 7, sc2tog; rep from * 1 more time. (16 sts)

Rnd 5: *Sc 2, sc2tog; rep from * 3 more times. (12 sts)

Rnds 6–8: Sc 12.

- Stuff shoe.

Rnd 9: Sc2tog 6 times. (6 sts)

- Fasten off and close hole in front of shoe.

TAIL

- In white, loosely ch 20 and join last chain to first chain with a slip stitch to form a ring.

Rnd 1: Sc 3, sl st 7, sc 3, hdc 7. (20 sts)

Rnd 2: Sc2tog 3 times, sl st 2, sc2tog 4 times, hdc 2, sc2tog 1 time. (12 sts)

Rnd 3: Sc2tog 6 times. (6 sts)

Rnd 4: In flo; *(sl st 1, ch 5, sl st in sc at base of ch-5) in next st, sk 1; rep from * 2 more times. (3 ch-5 lps)

- Fasten off, leaving a long tail for sewing. Using leftover yarn tail, cinch the space in the middle of rnd 4 closed by applying a running stitch around rnd 3.

ASSEMBLY

1. Sew the sewn edge of the bottom beak to the bottom edge of the top beak. (Fig. A–page 28)

2. Fold and attach the ends of the beak sides to the top and bottom corners of the top and bottom beak. (Fig. B–page 28)

3. Stuff and attach the beak to the lower half of the head. Stuff and close the seam. To help give the beak a flat shape, sew a line of running stitches 1 row in from the front edge of the beak through the top and bottom beak pieces. (Fig. C–page 28)

4. Flatten the bow piece and wrap the yarn tail tightly around the center to shape the bow and secure.

5. Cut out 2 eyes from light blue felt, 2 pupils and 2 eyelashes from black felt, and 2 eyelids from purple felt using templates. Assemble and glue or sew the eyes, eyelids, and eyelashes together before gluing or sewing the eyes to the head. Draw long stitches of black yarn along the crease between the top and bottom beak pieces. Sew eyebrows above the eyes. Attach the bow to the top of the head. (Fig. A)

6. Sew the crest down the back of the head. (Fig. B)

7. Sew the open ends of the fingers to the ends of the hands.

8. Sew the open end of the head to the open end of the body. Sew the arms to the body at the shoulders.

9. With the tapered end of the shoe at the front, sew the end of the leg onto the top of the shoe and sew the foot top detail to the top of the shoe and the front edge of the leg. Sew the heel to the bottom of the shoe. Sew top of leg to the body. (Fig. C)

10. Position the tail against the lower back of the body and rotate so the hdc stitches are at the bottom of the piece. Pin and sew the open edge of the tail to the lower portion of the body. Stuff before closing seam.

project
5

GOOFY

Tall and lovable Goofy! Who can resist laughing out loud at Goofy's haphazard cartoon instructional shorts like *The Art of Skiing* and *Goofy Gymnastics*? What he lacks in smarts he more than makes up for with his super positive attitude!

WHAT YOU'LL NEED

- G/6 (4mm) crochet hook
- Worsted weight yarn in green, black, beige, white, orange, blue, and brown
- Metal tapestry needle
- Black felt
- Fabric glue or needle and thread
- Stuffing

FINISHED SIZE: About 11" tall.

INSTRUCTIONS

HEAD

• In beige, loosely ch 10.

Rnd 1: Starting in second chain from hook and working in back ridge loops, sc 8, sc 3 in next st. Rotate chain so front loops are facing up. Starting in next st and working in front loops, sc 7, sc 2 in next st. (20 sts)

Rnd 2: *Sc 3, sc 2 in next st; rep from * 4 more times. (25 sts)

Rnds 3–6: Sc 25.

Rnd 7: *Sc 3, sc2tog; rep from * 4 more times. (20 sts)

Rnd 8: Sc 20.

Rnd 9: *Sc 3, sc2tog; rep from * 3 more times. (16 sts)

Rnd 10: Sc2tog 8 times. (8 sts)

• Change to black.

Rnd 11: Sc 2 in each st around. (16 sts)

Rnd 12: *Sc 7, sc 2 in next st; rep from * 1 more time. (18 sts)

Rnd 13: *Sc 5, sc 2 in next st; rep from * 2 more times. (21 sts)

Rnd 14: *Sc 6, sc 2 in next st; rep from * 2 more times. (24 sts)

Rnd 15: *Sc 5, sc 2 in next st; rep from * 3 more times. (28 sts)

Rnd 16: *Sc 6, sc 2 in next st; rep from * 3 more times. (32 sts)

Rnd 17: Sc 32.

Rnd 18: Sc2tog 16 times. (16 sts)

Rnd 19: *Sc 2, sc2tog; rep from * 3 more times. (12 sts)

• Stuff head.

Rnd 20: Sc2tog 6 times. (6 sts)

• Fasten off, leaving a long tail for sewing.

CHIN

• In beige, loosely ch 5.

Rnd 1: Starting in second chain from hook and working in back ridge loops, sc 3, sc 3 in next st. Rotate chain so front loops are facing up. Starting in next st and working in front loops, sc 2, sc 2 in next st. (10 sts)

Rnds 2–3: Sc 10.

Rnd 4: *Sc 1, sc 2 in next st; rep from * 4 more times. (15 sts)

Rnd 5: Sc 15.

Rnd 6: *Sc 1, sc2tog; rep from * 4 more times. (10 sts)

Rnd 7: Hdc 5, sc 5. (10 sts)

• Stuff lightly. Fasten off, leaving a long tail for sewing.

NOSE

• In black, sc 6 in an adjustable ring.

Rnd 1: Sc 6.

Rnd 2: Sc2tog 3 times. (3 sts)

• Fasten off, leaving a long tail for sewing.

EYES

• In white, loosely ch 6.

Row 1: Starting in second chain from hook, sc 5, ch 1 and turn. (5 sts)

Row 2: Sk first ch, sc 2 in next st, sc 3, sc 2 in next st, ch 1 and turn. (7 sts)

Row 3: Sk first ch, sc 7, turn. (7 sts)

Row 4: Sl st 1, hdc 3 in next st, sl st 1, sk 1, sl st 1, hdc 3 in next st, sl st 1. (10 sts)

• Fasten off, leaving a long tail for sewing.

EYEBROW

• In black, loosely ch 20.

Row 1: Starting in second ch from hook, sc 4, hdc 4, sl st 3, hdc 4, sc 4. (19 sts)

• Fasten off, leaving a long tail for sewing.

HEAD BUMP

• In black, sc 8 in an adjustable ring.

Rnd 1: *Sc 1, sc 2 in next st; rep from * 3 more times. (12 sts)

Rnd 2: Sc 12.

• Fasten off, leaving a long tail for sewing.

EAR (MAKE 2)
• In black, loosely ch 10.
Row 1: Starting in third ch from hook, dc 3 in st, hdc 3, sc 2, sl st 2. (10 sts)
• Fasten off, leaving a long tail for sewing.

BODY
• In blue, sc 8 in an adjustable ring.
Rnd 1: Sc 2 in each st around. (16 sts)
Rnd 2: Sc 16.
Rnd 3: *Sc 3, sc 2 in next st; rep from * 3 more times. (20 sts)
Rnd 4: Sc 20.
Rnd 5: *Sc 3, sc 2 in next st; rep from * 4 more times. (25 sts)
• Change to orange.
Rnd 6: In blo; sc 25.
Rnd 7: Sc 25.
Rnd 8: *Sc 3, sc2tog; rep from * 4 more times. (20 sts)
Rnds 9–12: Sc 20.
Rnd 13: *Sc 3, sc2tog; rep from * 3 more times. (16 sts)
• Stuff body.
Rnd 14: Sc2tog 8 times. (8 sts)
Rnds 15–17: Sc 8.
• Change to black.
Rnd 18: Sc 8.
Rnd 19: *Sc 1, sc 2 in next st: rep from * 3 more times. (12 sts)
• Fasten off, leaving a long tail for sewing.

TURTLENECK COLLAR
• In orange, loosely ch 12.
Row 1: Starting in second ch from hook, sc 11.
• Fasten off, leaving a long tail for sewing.

HAND AND ARM (MAKE 2)
• In white, sc 6 in an adjustable ring.

Rnd 1: Sc 2 in each st around. (12 sts)
Rnds 2–3: Sc 12.
Rnd 4: *Sc 1, sc2tog; rep from * 3 more times. (8 sts)
• Stuff hand.
Rnd 5: Sc2tog 4 times.
• Change to orange.
Rnd 6: In flo; sc 2 in each st around. (8 sts)
Rnds 7–15: Sc 8.
Rnd 16: *Sc 2, sc2tog; rep from * 1 more time. (6 sts)
• Stuff arm. Flatten seam and sew closed, leaving a long tail for sewing.

FINGERS AND TEETH (MAKE 10)
• In white, sc 6 in an adjustable ring.
Rnd 1: Sc 6.
• Fasten off, leaving a long tail for sewing. Do not stuff.

LEG (MAKE 2)
• In blue, sc 10 in an adjustable ring.
Rnd 1: Hdc 2 in each st around. (20 sts)
Rnd 2: In blo; *sc 2, sc2tog; rep from * 4 more times. (15 sts)
Rnd 3: *Sc 3, sc2tog; rep from * 2 more times. (12 sts)
Rnds 4–7: Sc 12.
Rnd 8: *Sc 4, sc2tog; rep from * 1 more time. (10 sts)
Rnds 9–11: Sc 10.
Rnd 12: Sc 2, hdc 2, dc 2, hdc 2, sc 2. (10 sts)
• Fasten off, leaving a long tail for sewing.

SHOE (MAKE 2)
• In brown, sc 8 in an adjustable ring.
Rnd 1: Sc 2 in each st around. (16 sts)
Rnd 2: Sc 16.
Rnd 3: *Sc 7, sc 2 in next st; rep from * 1 more time. (18 sts)
Rnd 4: *Sc 7, sc2tog; rep from * 1 more time. (16 sts)
Rnd 5: *Sc 2, sc2tog; rep from * 3 more

times. (12 sts)

Rnds 6–10: Sc 12.

• Stuff shoe.

Rnd 11: Sc2tog 6 times. (6 sts)

• Fasten off and close hole in back of shoe.

HAT

• In green, loosely chain 7.

Rnd 1: Starting in second chain from hook and working in back ridge loops, sc 5, sc 3 in next st. Rotate chain so front loops are facing up. Starting in next st and working in front loops, sc 4, sc 2 in next st. (14 sts)

Rnd 2: *Sc 1, sc 2 in next st: rep from * 6 more times. (21 sts)

Rnds 3–4: Sc 21.

Rnd 5: Sc2tog 5 times, sc 1, sc2tog 5 times. (11 sts)

Rnd 6: In flo; sc 11.

Rnd 7: Sc 9, sc2tog. (10 sts)

Rnd 8: Sc 8, sc2tog. (9 sts)

Rnd 9: Sc 7, sc2tog. (8 sts)

• Stuff hat.

Rnd 10: In flo; *sc 1, sc 2 in next st; rep from * 3 more times. (12 sts)

Rnd 11: In blo; sc 12.

Rnd 12: Sl st 12.

• Fasten off, leaving a long tail for sewing.

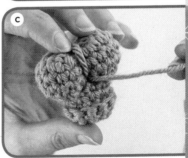

VEST

• In black, sc 8 in an adjustable ring.

Rnd 1: *Sc 1, sc 3 in next st; rep from * 3 more times. (16 sts)

Rnd 2: Sc 2, *sc 3 in next st, sc 3; rep from * 2 more times, sc 3 in next st, sc 1. (24 sts)

Rnd 3: Sc 3, sc 3 in next st, sc 5, (sc 2, pm, sc 1) in next st, sc 5, sc 3 in next st, sc 5, (sc 2, pm, sc 1) in next st, sc 2. (32 sts)

Rnd 4: Sl st 4, sc 2 in next st, ch 8, skip ahead and sc 2 in next pm st, sc 7, sc

2 in next st, ch 8, skip ahead and sc 2 in next pm st, sl st 3. Remove markers. (38 sts)

Rnd 5: Sl st 6, sc 8 in ch sp, hdc 3 in next st, hdc 9, hdc 3 in next st, sc 8 in ch sp, sl st 5. (42 sts)

• Fasten off, leaving a long tail for sewing.

ASSEMBLY

1. Attach the open end of the nose to the front of the head. Using black yarn, loop a long stitch through the front of the muzzle and into the roof of the mouth 2 to 3 times, pulling tightly to form the lip cleft. (Fig. A–page 39)

2. Sew the open edges of the teeth to the bottom front of the muzzle. Sew the eyes to the front of the head. Sew the eyebrows around the outside edge of the eyes. Sew the chin to the head at the back of the muzzle (stitch marker will indicate the bottom of the chin). To shape the lower lip, sew 2 to 3 running stitches through the bottom of the chin, into the muzzle, and back out through the chin roughly 1 row back from the front, pulling firmly. (Fig. B–page 39)

3. Fold the hat brim up from rnd 10 and secure with 2 to 3 stitches. Using a long stitch, loop yarn through and over the top portion of the hat 3 to 4 times. Pull tightly to shape the two halves of the top of the hat. (Fig. C–page 39)

4. Cut out 2 eye pupils from the black felt using template. Glue or sew the pupils to the eyes. Attach the ears to the sides of the head. Sew the open edge of the head bump to the back of the head and stuff before closing seam. Stuff hat lightly before sewing to the top of the head. Cut a $1/4$"-wide strip of black felt long enough to fit around the center column of the hat, and sew or glue in place. Using a single strand of black yarn, add a small bit of hair to the top of the head above the eyebrows. Separate the yarn plys with your tapestry needle and trim. Using black yarn run a long stitch along the crease of the mouth where the muzzle and chin come together. (Fig. D–page 39)

5. Sew the open ends of the fingers to the ends of the hands. Using black yarn, add 3 short stitches to the back of the hands. (Figs. E and Ee)

6. Sew the head to the neck. Sew the arms to the body at the shoulders. Insert the arms through the vest and secure the vest to the body. Sew collar around the last rnd of orange on the neck. (Fig. F)

7. Stuff legs and sew to the sides of the body with dc stitches at the top of the hips. With the larger, rounder end of the shoes in the front, sew the shoes to the bottom of the pants using blue yarn. (Fig. G)

PLUTO

Good ol' Pluto! Where would Mickey Mouse be without his faithful pup? Pluto looks equally dapper in either a green or red collar (or any other color you can think of)!

WHAT YOU'LL NEED

- G/6 (4mm) crochet hook
- Worsted weight yarn in yellow, black, and white
- Metal tapestry needle
- Black and green (or red) felt
- Fabric glue or needle and thread
- Stuffing

FINISHED SIZE: About 5" tall.

INSTRUCTIONS

HEAD

- In yellow, loosely ch 8.

Rnd 1: Starting in second chain from hook and working in back ridge loops, sc 6, sc 3 in next st. Rotate chain so front loops are facing up. Starting in next st and working in front loops, sc 5, sc 2 in next st. (16 sts)

Rnd 2: *Sc 3, sc 2 in next st; rep from * 3 more times. (20 sts)

Rnds 3–5: Sc 20.

Rnd 6: *Sc 3, sc2tog; rep from * 3 more times. (16 sts)

Rnd 7: Sc 16.

- Stuff muzzle.

Rnd 8: Sc2tog 8 times. (8 sts)

Rnd 9: Sc 2 in each st around. (16 sts)

Rnd 10: *Sc 7, sc 2 in next st; rep from * 1 more time. (18 sts)

Rnd 11: Sc 18.

Rnd 12: *Sc 5, sc 2 in next st; rep from * 2 more times. (21 sts)

Rnd 13: *Sc 6, sc 2 in next st; rep from * 2 more times. (24 sts)

Rnd 14: *Sc 5, sc 2 in next st; rep from * 3 more times. (28 sts)

Rnd 15: *Sc 6, sc 2 in next st; rep from * 3 more times. (32 sts)

Rnd 16: Sc 32.

Rnd 17: Sc2tog 16 times. (16 sts)

Rnd 18: *Sc 2, sc2tog; rep from * 3 more times. (12 sts)

- Stuff head.

Rnd 19: Sc2tog 6 times. (6 sts)

- Fasten off, leaving a long tail.

CHIN

- In yellow, loosely ch 5.

Rnd 1: Starting in second chain from hook and working in back ridge loops, sc 3, sc 3 in next st. Rotate chain so front loops are facing up. Starting in next st and working in front loops, sc 2, sc 2 in next st. (10 sts)

Rnds 2–3: Sc 10.

Rnd 4: *Sc 1, sc 2 in next st; rep from * 4 more times. (15 sts)

Rnd 5: Sc 15.

Rnd 6: *Sc 1, sc2tog; rep from * 4 more times. (10 sts)

Rnd 7: Hdc 3, pm, hdc 2, sc 5. (10 sts)

- Stuff lightly. Fasten off, leaving a long tail for sewing.

NOSE

- In black, sc 6 in an adjustable ring.

Rnd 1: Sc 6.

Rnd 2: Sc2tog 3 times. (3 sts)

- Fasten off, leaving a long tail for sewing.

EYES

- In white, loosely ch 6.

Row 1: Starting in second chain from hook, sc 5, ch 1 and turn. (5 sts)

Row 2: Sk first ch, sc 2 in next st, sc 3, sc 2 in next st, ch 1 and turn. (7 sts)

Row 3: Sk first ch, sc 7, turn. (7 sts)

Row 4: Sl st 1, hdc 3 in next st, sl st 1, sk 1, sl st 1, hdc 3 in next st, sl st 1. (10 sts)

- Fasten off, leaving a long tail for sewing.

EYEBROW

- In yellow, loosely ch 20.

Row 1: Starting in second ch from hook, sc 4, hdc 4, sl st 3, hdc 4, sc 4. (19 sts)

- Fasten off, leaving a long tail for sewing.

HEAD BUMP

- in yellow, sc 8 in an adjustable ring.

Rnd 1: *Sc 1, sc 2 in next st; rep from * 3 more times. (12 sts)

Rnd 2: Sc 12.

- Fasten off, leaving a long tail for sewing.

EAR (MAKE 2)

- In black, loosely ch 14.

Row 1: Dc 3 in third ch from hook, hdc 4, sc 4, sl st 3. (14 sts)

- Fasten off, leaving a long tail for sewing.

BODY

- In yellow, sc 10 in an adjustable ring.

Rnd 1: Sc 2 in each st around. (20 sts)

Rnd 2: Sc 20.

Rnd 3: *Sc 3, sc 2 in next st; rep from * 4 more times. (25 sts)

Rnds 4–6: Sc 25.

Rnd 7: *Sc 3, sc2tog; rep from * 4 more times. (20 sts)

Rnd 8: Sc 20.

Rnd 9: *Sc 3, sc2tog; rep from * 3 more times. (16 sts)

Rnds 10–11: Sc 16.

Rnd 12: *Sc 1, sc 2 in next st; rep from * 7 more times. (24 sts)

Rnd 13: Sc 24.

Rnd 14: Sc2tog 12 times.

- Stuff body.

Rnd 15: Sc2tog 6 times.

- Fasten off, leaving a long tail for sewing.

NECK

- In yellow, loosely ch 12 and join last chain to first chain with a slip stitch to form a ring.

Rnd 1: Sc 12.

Rnd 2: *Sc 1, sc2tog; rep from * 3 more times. (8 sts)

Rnds 3–4: Sc 8.

Rnd 5: *Sc 3, sc 2 in next st; rep from * 1 more time. (10 sts)

- Fasten off, leaving a long tail for sewing.

LEG (MAKE 4)

• In yellow, sc 10 in an adjustable ring.
Rnd 1: Sc 2, sc 2 in next st, hdc 2 in next st, dc 2 in next 2 sts, hdc 2 in next st, sc 2 in next st, sc 2. (16 sts)
Rnd 2: Sc 5, hdc 6, sc 5. (16 sts)
Rnd 3: Sc 3, sc2tog 5 times, sc 3. (11 sts)
Rnds 4–9: Sc 11.
• Partially stuff leg.
Rnd 10: Sc 9, sc2tog. (10 sts)
Rnd 11: Sc 8, sc2tog. (9 sts)
Rnd 12: Sc 7, sc2tog. (8 sts)
• Finish stuffing leg.
• Fasten off, leaving a long tail for sewing. Flatten open edge and sew closed.

TAIL

• In black, make a 2″ long twisted cord.

ASSEMBLY

1. Attach the open end of the nose to the front of the head. Using black yarn, loop a long stitch through the front of the muzzle and into the roof of the mouth 2 to 3 times, pulling tightly to form the lip cleft. (Fig. A)

2. Sew the eyes to the front of the head. Sew the eyebrows around the outside edge of the eyes. Sew the open edge of the chin to the head at the back of the muzzle (stitch marker will indicate the bottom of chin). To shape and secure the lower lip, sew 2 to 3 running stitches through the bottom of the chin, into the muzzle, and back out through the chin, roughly 1 row back from the front, pulling firmly. (Fig. B)

3. Cut out 2 eye pupils from black felt using template. Glue or sew the pupils to the eyes. Sew the open edge of the

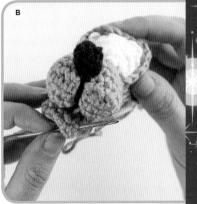

head bump to the back of the head and stuff before closing the seam. Attach the ears to the sides of the head. Using black yarn, run a long stitch along the outline of the mouth where the muzzle and chin come together. (Fig. C-page 45)

4. Sew the larger end of the neck to the larger end of the body and stuff. Sew the head to the top of the neck. Cut a $3/4"$ wide by $3"$ long strip of green or red felt. Fold the long way and glue or sew the long edges together. Wrap the collar around the neck and sew the short ends together. (Fig. D)

5. Using black yarn, shape the toes by looping a long stitch 1 to 2 times through the front of the foot twice. Repeat on the other 3 legs. (Fig. E)

6. Sew the legs to the sides of the body. To keep the legs from splaying out, attach yellow yarn to the inside surface of one leg, pass the yarn through the body to the inside surface of the opposite leg, then back again through the body to the starting point. Pull gently to draw the legs close to the body. Attach the tail to the back of the body. (Fig. F)

CHIP 'N' DALE

These two mischievous chipmunks love their peanuts and acorns almost as much as they love playing practical jokes on their friends—especially Pluto and Donald. Be sure to keep an eye on them, or they may get into trouble!

WHAT YOU'LL NEED

- G/6 (4mm) crochet hook
- Worsted weight yarn in light brown, medium brown, white, black, beige, and dark red
- Metal tapestry needle
- White and black felt
- Fabric glue or needle and thread
- Stuffing

FINISHED SIZE: About 7" tall.

INSTRUCTIONS

HEAD

- In light brown (Dale) or medium brown (Chip), sc 8 in an adjustable ring.

Rnd 1: Sc 2 in each st around. (16 sts)

Rnd 2: Sc 16.

Rnd 3: *Sc 3, sc 2 in next st; rep from * 3 more times. (20 sts)

Rnd 4: Sc 20.

Rnd 5: *Sc 1, sc 2 in next st; rep from * 9 more times. (30 sts)

Rnd 6: Sc 30.

Rnd 7: *Sc 4, sc 2 in next st; rep from * 5 more times. (36 sts)

Rnd 8: Sc 36.

Rnd 9: *Sc 1, sc2tog; rep from * 11 more times. (24 sts)

Rnd 10: Sc 24.

Rnd 11: *Sc 1, sc2tog; rep from * 7 more times. (16 sts)

Rnd 12: Sc 16.

- Stuff head.

Rnd 13: Sc2tog 8 times. (8 sts)

- Fasten off, leaving a long tail for sewing.

BODY

- In light brown (Dale) or medium brown (Chip), sc 10 in an adjustable ring.

Rnd 1: Sc 2 in each st around. (20 sts)

Rnd 2: Sc 20.

Rnd 3: *Sc 1, sc 2 in next st; rep from * 9 more times. (30 sts)

Rnds 4–6: Sc 30.

Rnd 7: *Sc 1, sc2tog; rep from * 9 more times. (20 sts)

Rnd 8: Sc 20.

Rnd 9: *Sc 3, sc2tog; rep from * 3 more times. (16 sts)

Rnd 10: *Sc 1, sc 2 in next st; rep from * 7 more times. (24 sts)

Rnd 11: Sc 24.

Rnd 12: Sc2tog 12 times.

- Stuff body.

Rnd 13: Sc2tog 6 times.

- Fasten off, leaving a long tail for sewing.

CHEEKS AND EYESPOTS

- In beige, loosely ch 11.

Rnd 1: Starting in second chain from hook and working in back ridge loops, sc 9, sc 3 in next st. Rotate chain so front loops are facing up. Starting in next st and working in front loops, sc 8, sc 2 in next st. (22 sts)

Rnd 2: Hdc 2 in next st, sl st 8, hdc 2 in next 3 st, sc 8, hdc 2 in next 2 st. (28 sts)

Rnd 3: Hdc 2 in next 2 sts, sl st 8, hdc 2 in next 6 st, sc 8, hdc 2 in next 4 st. (40 sts)

Rnd 4: Sc2tog 3 times, sl st 6, sc2tog 7 times, sc 6, sc2tog 4 times. (26 sts)

- Count 2 sts (A) and 8 sts (B) away from hook and apply a pm to these stitches. Work the eyespots with RS facing you. Once markers are placed, cut and fasten off yarn, leaving a long tail for sewing.

CREATE LEFT EYESPOT.

- With RS facing you, start working in pm st "A" on left side of face.

Row 1: To rejoin beige yarn; (sl st 1, ch 1, sc 1) in pm st, sc 1, hdc 2, ch 2 and turn. Remove marker (A). (4 sts)

Row 2: Sk first and second ch, hdc 2, sc 2, ch 1 and turn. (4 sts)

Row 3: Sk first ch, sk 1, hdc 3 in next 2 sts, sl st 1. (8 sts)

- Fasten off yarn in next st, leaving a long tail for sewing.

CREATE RIGHT EYESPOT.

- With RS facing you, start working in pm st "B" on right side of face.

Row 1: To rejoin beige yarn; (sl st 1, ch

2, hdc) in pm st, hdc 1, sc 2, ch 1 and turn. Remove marker (B). (4 sts)

Row 2: Sk first ch, sc 2, hdc 2, ch 1 and turn. (4 sts)

Row 3: Sk first ch, sk 1, hdc 3 in next 2 sts, sl st 1.

• Fasten off yarn in next st and cut, leaving a long tail for sewing.

MUZZLE

• In white, sc 6 in an adjustable ring.

Rnd 1: *Sc 1, sc 2 in next st; rep from * 2 more times. (9 sts)

Rnd 2: *Sc 2, sc 2 in next st; rep from * 2 more times. (12 sts)

Rnd 3: *Sc 1, sc 2 in next st; rep from * 5 more times. (18 sts)

Rnd 4: *Sc 1, sc2tog; rep from * 5 more times. (12 sts)

• Fasten off, leaving a long tail for sewing.

CHIP NOSE

• In black, sc 4 in an adjustable ring and fasten off, leaving a long tail for sewing.

DALE NOSE

• In red, sc 4 in an adjustable ring.

Rnd 1: *Sc 1, sc 2 in next st; rep from * 1 more time. (6 sts)

Rnd 2: Sc 6.

Rnd 3: *Sc 1, sc2tog; rep from * 1 more time. (4 sts)

• Fasten off and stuff lightly before closing hole.

EAR (MAKE 2)

• In light brown (Dale) or medium brown (Chip), sc 6 in an adjustable ring. Do not join last st to first st. Ch 1 and turn.

Row 1: Sk first ch, sl st 2, (sc 1, hdc 1) in next st, (hdc 1, sc 1) in next st, sl st 2.

• Fasten off, leaving a long tail for sewing.

LEG (MAKE 2)

• In light brown (Dale) or medium brown (Chip), sc 8 in an adjustable ring.

Rnd 1: Sc 8. (8 sts)

Rnd 2: Sc 2 in each st around. (16 sts)

Rnd 3: *Sc 7, sc 2 in next st; rep from * 1 more time. (18 sts)

Rnds 4–5: Sc 18.

• Fasten off, leaving a long tail for sewing.

FOOT (MAKE 2)

• In light brown (Dale) or medium brown (Chip), sc 4 in an adjustable ring.

Rnd 1: Sc 2 in each st around. (8 sts)

Rnd 2: *Sc 1, sc 2 in next st; rep from * 3 more times. (12 sts)

Rnd 3: *Sc 2, sc 2 in next st; rep from * 3 more times. (16 sts)

Rnd 4: *Sc 2, sc2tog; rep from * 3 more times. (12 sts)

Rnds 5–8: Sc 12.

• Stuff foot.

Rnd 9: *Sc 1, sc2tog; rep from * 3 more times. (8 sts)

Rnd 10: Sc2tog 4 times. (4 sts)

• Fasten off and close hole in back of foot.

HAND AND ARM (MAKE 2)

• In light brown (Dale) or medium brown (Chip), sc 6 in an adjustable ring.

Rnd 1: Sc 2 in each st around. (12 sts)

Rnds 2–3: Sc 12.

Rnd 4: *Sc 1, sc2tog; rep from * 3 more times. (8 sts)

• Stuff hand.

Rnd 5: *Sc 2, sc2tog; rep from * 1 more time. (6 sts)

Rnd 6: *Sc 2, sc 2 in next st; rep from * 1 more time. (8 sts)

Rnds 7–8: Sc 8.

• Stuff arm.

Rnd 9: *Sc 2, sc2tog; rep from * 1 more time. (6 sts)
• Flatten seam and sew closed, leaving a long tail for sewing.

TAIL
• In black, loosely ch 16.
Rnd 1: Starting in second chain from hook and working in back ridge loops, sl st 14, sc 3 in next st. Rotate chain so front loops are facing up. Starting in next st and working in front loops, sl st 14. (31 sts)
• Change to white yarn.
Rnd 2: In blo; sc 3 in next st, sl st 4, sc 5, sl st 5, tbl; (sc 1, hdc 1, dc 1, hdc 1, sc 1) in next st, in blo; sl st 5, sc 5, sl st 4, sc 3 in next st. (39 sts)
• Fasten off, leaving a long tail for sewing.

BELLY
• In beige, loosely ch 8.
Rnd 1: Starting in second chain from hook and working in back ridge loops, sc 1, hdc 2, sc 1, hdc 2, hdc 3 in next st. Rotate chain so front loops are facing up. Starting in next st and working in front loops, hdc 2, sc 1, hdc 2, sc 2 in next st. (16 sts)
Rnd 2: Sc 2 in next st, hdc 2, sc 1, hdc 2, hdc 2 in next 3 sts, hdc 2, sc 1, hdc 2, sc 2 in next 2 sts. (22 sts)
Rnd 3: Sc 2 in next 2 sts, sc 2, sl st 1, sc 2, hdc 6, sc 2, sl st 1, sc 2, sc 2 in next 4 sts. (28 sts)
• Fasten off, leaving a long tail for sewing.

ASSEMBLY

1. Position the cheeks on the lower half of the head and pin in place. Sew completely around the cheeks and stuff before closing the seam. Sew the

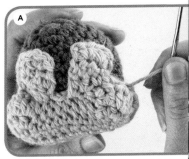

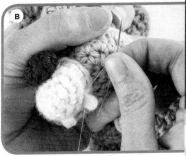

eye patches down, leaving roughly 2 sts worth of space between them. (Fig. A–page 51)

2. Sew the open edge of the muzzle to the top half of the cheeks between the eyes, and stuff before closing seam. Attach the nose.

For Dale only: Turn the larger red nose shape on its side and sew the nose to the upper front of the muzzle. Cut out 2 teeth from white felt using template. Glue or sew the back half of the 2 teeth to Dale's muzzle. (Fig. B–page 51)

For Chip only: Attach smaller black nose to the upper front of the muzzle. Using white yarn, loop a long stitch through the bottom half of the muzzle 2–3 times, pulling tightly to form the lip cleft. Cut out 1 tooth from white felt using template. Glue or sew the back half of the tooth to Chip's muzzle. (Fig. C–page 51)

3. Cut out two eyes from white felt and 2 pupils from black felt using templates. Assemble and glue or sew the eyes together before gluing or sewing the eyes to the eyespots. Attach the ears at the top of the head. (Fig. D–page 51)

For Dale only: Attach a fringe of 4 to 5 pieces of 4" light brown yarn to the top of the head. Separate the yarn plys with a tapestry needle and trim as desired. (Fig. E)

4. Using black yarn, form the fingers and toes by looping a long stitch of yarn 1 to 2 times through the front of the feet and 3 times through the front of the hands. (Fig. F)

5. Sew the open edge of the head to the open edge of the body. Sew the open edges of the legs to the lower corners of the body at the hips. Stuff before closing the seam. With the larger, rounder ends of the feet at the front, attach the tops of the feet to the bottom portion of the legs. Attach the arms at the shoulders. Attach the belly directly below the chin and sew to the front of the body. (Fig. G–page 52)

6. Using the leftover white yarn tail, attach the tail to the back of the neck and down the back, leaving the end free. (Fig. H–page 52)

project
8

DUMBO

It's a bird! It's a plane! It's a . . . flying pachyderm! Who can resist this cute and cuddly baby elephant as he flies by to say hello? Be sure to stock up on peanuts if you invite this little guy into your home.

WHAT YOU'LL NEED

- G/6 (4mm) and E/4 (3.5 mm) crochet hooks
- Worsted weight yarn in gray, pink, white, red, yellow, and black
- Metal tapestry needle
- Black, light blue, and white felt
- Fabric glue or needle and thread
- Stuffing

FINISHED SIZE: About 5" tall.

INSTRUCTIONS

HEAD

• In gray, sc 8 in an adjustable ring.
Rnd 1: In blo; sc 8.
Rnds 2–3: Sc 8.
Rnd 4: *Sc 1, sc 2 in next st; rep from * 3 more times. (12 sts)
Rnd 5: Sc 12.
Rnds 6–7: Sc 2, hdc 2, dc 4, hdc 2, sc 2. (12 sts)
Rnd 8: In flo; hdc 2 in next 2 sts, sc 2 in next 8 sts, hdc 2 in next 2 sts. (24 sts)
Rnd 9: Hdc 2 in next 6 sts, sc 12, hdc 2 in next 6 sts. (36 sts)
Rnd 10: Sc2tog 6 times, sc 12, sc2tog 6 times. (24 sts)
Rnd 11: Sc 8, hdc 2, dc 4, hdc 2, sc 8. (24 sts)
Rnd 12: *Sc 1, sc 2 in next st; rep from * 3 more times, hdc 2, dc 4, hdc 2, **sc 2 in next st, sc 1; rep from ** 3 more times. (32 sts)
Rnd 13: Sc 12, hdc 2, dc 4, hdc 2, sc 12. (32 sts)
Rnd 14: *Sc 1, sc2tog; rep from * 3 more times, sc 8, **sc2tog, sc 1; rep from ** 3 more times. (24 sts)
Rnds 15–16: Sc 24.
Rnd 17: *Sc 2, sc2tog; rep from * 5 more times. (18 sts)
Rnd 18: *Sc 1, sc2tog; rep from * 5 more times. (12 sts)
• Stuff head.
Rnd 19: Sc2tog 6 times. (6 sts)
• Fasten off, leaving a long tail for sewing.

LOWER LIP

• In gray, sc 6 in an adjustable ring. Do not join last st to first st. Ch 1 and turn.
Row 1: Sk first ch, sl st 6.
• Fasten off, leaving a long tail for sewing.

BODY

• In gray, sc 10 in an adjustable ring.
Rnd 1: Sc 2 in each st around. (20 sts)
Rnd 2: *Sc 3, sc 2 in next st; rep from * 4 more times. (25 sts)
Rnd 3: Sc 25.
Rnd 4: *Sc 4, sc 2 in next st; rep from * 4 more times. (30 sts)
Rnds 5–7: Sc 30.
Rnd 8: *Sc 1, sc2tog; rep from * 9 more times. (20 sts)
Rnds 9–10: Sc 20.
Rnd 11: *Sc 3, sc2tog; rep from * 3 more times. (16 sts)
Rnd 12: Sc 16.
• Stuff body.
Rnd 13: Sc2tog 8 times. (8 sts)
• Fasten off, leaving a long tail for sewing.

LEG (MAKE 4)

• In gray, sc 6 in an adjustable ring.
Rnd 1: Hdc 2 in each st around. (12 sts)
Rnd 2: In blo; sc 12.
Rnds 3–5: Sc 12.
Rnd 6: *Sc 4, sc2tog; rep from * 1 more time. (10 sts)
Rnd 7: Sc 10.
• Stuff leg.
Rnd 8: Sc2tog 5 times. (5 sts)
• Fasten off, leaving a long tail for sewing. Flatten open edges and sew closed.

RIGHT EAR

• In gray, sc 8 in an adjustable ring.
Rnd 1: Sc 2 in each st around. (16 sts)
Rnd 2: Sc 2 in next 4 sts, sc 4, hdc 2 in next 3 sts, sc 2 in next 2 sts, sc 3. (25 sts)
Rnd 3: Sc 2, sc 2 in next st, sc 4, hdc 2 in next st, dc 2 in next st, hdc 1, sc 3, dc 2 in next 2 sts, hdc 2, sc 8. (30 sts)
Rnd 4: Sc 9, hdc 3 in next st, dc 3 in next st, hdc 1, sc 1, sl st 4, hdc 2 in next st, dc 2 in next 4 sts, sc 3, sl st 5. (39 sts)

Rnd 5: Sl st 23, hdc 2 in next st, dc 2 in next 4 sts, sc 4, sl st 7. (44 sts)

Rnd 6: Sl st 23, hdc 2 in next 3 sts, dc 2 in next 5 sts, hdc 2 in next 2 sts, sc 4, sl st 7. (54 sts)

• Fasten off, leaving a long tail for sewing.

LEFT EAR

• In gray, sc 8 in an adjustable ring.

Rnd 1: Sc 2 in each st around. (16 sts)

Rnd 2: Sc 3, sc 2 in next 2 sts, hdc 2 in next 3 sts, sc 4, sc 2 in next 4 sts. (25 sts)

Rnd 3: Sc 8, hdc 2, dc 2 in next 2 sts, sc 3, hdc 1, dc 2 in next st, hdc 2 in next st, sc 4, sc 2 in next st, sc 2. (30 sts)

Rnd 4: Sl st 5, sc 3, dc 2 in next 4 sts, hdc 2 in next st, sl st 4, sc 1, hdc 1, dc 3 in next st, hdc 3 in next st, sc 9. (39 sts)

Rnd 5: Sl st 7, sc 4, dc 2 in next 4 sts, hdc 2 in next st, sl st 23. (44 sts)

Rnd 6: Sl st 7, sc 4, hdc 2 in next 2 sts, dc 2 in next 5 sts, hdc 2 in next 3 st, sl st 23. (54 sts)

• Fasten off, leaving a long tail for sewing.

INNER EARS

• In pink, make 1 more left and right ear using a size E/4 (3.5 mm) hook. Leave a long tail for sewing after fastening off.

COLLAR

• In red, loosely ch 15 and join last chain to first chain with a slip stitch to form a ring.

Rnd 1: Sc 3 in each st. (42 sts)

• Change to yellow.

Rnd 2: Sc 2 in each st. (84 sts)

• Change to red.

Rnd 3: In flo; sl st 84.

• Fasten off yarn and work in the yarn tails.

HAT

• In yellow, sc 6 in an adjustable ring.

Rnd 1: Sc 6.

Rnd 2: *Sc 2, sc 2 in next st; rep from * 1 more time. (8 sts)

Rnds 3–5: Sc 8.

Rnd 6: In flo; *sc 1, sc 2 in next st; rep from * 3 more times. (12 sts)

Rnd 7: In flo; sc 12.

Rnd 8: In blo; *sc 1, sc 2 in next st; rep from * 5 more times. (18 sts)

• Fasten off.

TAIL

• In gray, make a 1" long twisted cord.

ASSEMBLY

1. Place the WS of the pink inner ear against the RS of the gray outer ear. Using pink yarn, attach the inner ear to only the inside surface of the outer ear using a running stitch. Shape the ear by folding the top corner closest to the head over and secure the shaping with gray yarn. (Fig. A)

2. Close the hole in the back of the head. Sew the open end of the body to the bottom of the head. Work the collar up the body until it reaches the neck. Sew the back edge of the lower lip to where the trunk meets the head. (Fig. B)

3. Cut out 2 eyes from white felt, 2 irises from light blue felt, and 2 pupils from black felt using template. Glue or sew the felt pieces together before gluing or sewing the eyes to the front of the head. Using black yarn, add 2 eyelashes above each eye and 2 short parallel stitches for eyebrows 2 to 3 rows above the eyes. Attach the ears

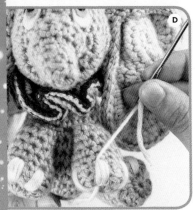

to the sides of the head. Fold the brim of the hat up from rnd 6. Stuff and sew the hat to the head. Using a single strand of black yarn, add a small bit of hair to the top of the head. Separate the yarn plys with your tapestry needle and trim. (Fig. C–page 57)

4. Sew the legs to the body at the shoulders and hips. To help keep the legs from splaying out, sew the inside surfaces of the legs to the body as well. Embroider 3 groupings of 5 white stitches to the front of each foot for toenails. (Fig. D)

5. Attach the tail to the back of the body. (Fig. E)

TIP: *Does your Dumbo need a magic feather? Use the feather template to send him soaring!*

BAMBI

This sweet fawn, Bambi, with his delicate legs and flashy spots, loves to bound and jump with his forest friends. He's the most graceful deer around—at least, until you get him on an icy pond.

WHAT YOU'LL NEED

- G/6 (4mm) crochet hook
- Worsted weight yarn in orange, reddish-orange, pink, beige, and black
- Metal tapestry needle
- White, black, reddish-orange, brown, and beige felt
- Fabric glue or needle and thread
- Stuffing

FINISHED SIZE: About 8" tall.

INSTRUCTIONS

SIDE (MAKE 2)

• In orange, loosely ch 4.

Row 1: Starting in second ch from hook, sc 3, ch 1 and turn. (3 sts)

Rows 2–3: Sk first ch, sc 3, ch 1 and turn. (3 sts)

Row 4: Sk first ch, sc 1, sc 2 in next st, sc 1, ch 1 and turn. (4 sts)

Row 5: Sk first ch, sc 4, ch 12 and turn. (16 sts)

Row 6: Starting in second ch from hook, sc 15, ch 1 and turn. (15 sts)

Rows 7–8: Sk first ch, sc 15, ch 1 and turn. (15 sts)

Row 9: Sk first ch, sc2tog, sc11, sc2tog, ch 1 and turn. (13 sts)

Row 10: Sk first ch, sc 13, ch 1 and turn. (13 sts)

Row 11: Sk first ch, sc 1, pm, sc 12, ch 1 and turn. (13 sts)

START BACK LEG

Row 12: Sk first ch, sc 2 in next st, sc 3, ch 1 and turn. (5 sts)

Row 13: Sk first ch, sc2tog, sc 2, sc 2 in next st ch 1 and turn. (5 sts)

Row 14: Sk first ch, sc 2 in next st, sc2tog twice, ch 1 and turn. (4 sts)

Row 15: Sk first ch, sc2tog, sc 2, ch 1 and turn. (3 sts)

Rows 16–21: Sk first ch, sc 3, ch 1 and turn. (3 sts)

Row 22: Sk first ch, sc 3, change to black, ch 1 and turn. (3 sts)

Rows 23–24: Sk first ch, sc 3, ch 1 and turn. (3 sts)

Row 25: Sk first ch, sc 1, sk 1, sc 1. (2 sts)

• Fasten off black yarn, leaving a long tail for sewing.

START FRONT LEG

Row 12: To rejoin orange yarn; (sl st 1, ch 1, sc 1) in pm st, sc 4, ch 1 and turn.

Remove marker. (5 sts)

Row 13: Sk first ch, sc2tog, sc 3, ch 1 and turn. (4 sts)

Row 14: Sk first ch, sc2tog, sc 2, ch 1 and turn. (3 sts)

Rows 15–22: Sk first ch, sc 3, ch 1 and turn. (3 sts)

• Change to black.

Rows 23–24: Sk first ch, sc 3, ch 1 and turn. (3 sts)

Row 25: Sk first ch, sc 1, sk 1, sc 1. (2 sts)

• Fasten off black yarn, leaving a long tail for sewing.

BELLY

• In beige, loosely ch 4 sts.

Row 1: Starting in second ch from hook, sc 3, ch 1 and turn.

Rows 2–7: Sk first ch, sc 3, ch 1 and turn. (3 sts)

Row 8: Sk first ch, sc 1, sc 2 in next st, sc 1, ch 1 and turn. (4 sts)

Row 9: Sk first ch, sc 4, ch 1 and turn. (4 sts)

Row 10: Sk first ch, sc 1, sc 2 in next 2 sts, sc 1, ch 1 and turn. (6 sts)

Row 11: Sk first ch, sc 6, ch 1 and turn. Pm on the edges at beginning and end of this row. (6 sts)

Rows 12–14: Sk first ch, sc 6, ch 1 and turn. (6 sts)

Row 15: Sk first ch, sc 2, sc2tog, sc 2, ch 1 and turn. Pm on the edges at beginning and end of this row. (5 sts)

Rows 16–17: Sk first ch, sc 5, ch 1 and turn. (5 sts)

Row 18: Sk first ch, sc 1, sc 2 in next 3 sts, sc 1, ch 1 and turn. (8 sts)

Row 19: Sk first ch, sc 8, ch 1 and turn. (8 sts)

Row 20: Sk first ch, sc 8, ch 1 and turn. Pm on the edges at beginning and end of this row. (8 sts)

Rows 21–22: Sk first ch, sc 8, ch 1 and turn. (8 sts)

Row 23: Sk first ch, sc 1, sc2tog 3 times, sc 1, ch 1 and turn. (5 sts)

Row 24: Sk first ch, sc 5, ch 1 and turn. Pm on the edges at beginning and end of this row. (5 sts)

Rows 25–26: Sk first ch, sc 5, ch 1 and turn. (5 sts)

Row 27: Sk first ch, sc 2, sk 1, sc 2, ch 1 and turn. (4 sts)

Row 28: Sk first ch, sc 4, ch 1 and turn. (4 sts)

Row 29: Sk first ch, sc 1, sc2tog, sc 1, ch 1 and turn. (3 sts)

Rows 30–31: Sk first ch, sc 3, ch 1 and turn. (3 sts)

Row 32: Sk first ch, sc 1, sc 2 in next st, sc 1, ch 1 and turn. (4 sts)

Row 33: Sk first ch, sc 1, sc 2 in next 2 sts, sc 1, ch 1 and turn. (6 sts)

Row 34: Sk first ch, sc 6, ch 1 and turn. (6 sts)

Row 35: Sk first ch, sc2tog, sc 2, sc2tog, ch 1 and turn. (4 sts)

Row 36: Sk first ch, sc2tog 2 times, ch 1 and turn. (2 sts)

Row 37: Sk first ch, sc2tog. (1 sts)

- Fasten off, leaving a long tail for sewing.
- Before beginning on legs, select a side of your belly piece to be the RS and secure a pm to this side.

LEFT FRONT LEG

Row 1: With RS facing up, in orange work along the edge from the row 15 pm toward the row 11 pm. To rejoin beige yarn; (sl st 1, ch 1, sc 1) in row 15 pm st, sc 4 to row 11 pm st, ch 1 and turn. Remove these markers. (5 sts)

Row 2: Sk first ch, sc2tog, sc 3, ch 1 and turn. (4 sts)

Row 3: Sk first ch, sc2tog, sc 2, change to orange, ch 1 and turn. (3 sts)

Rows 4–10: Sk first ch, sc 3, ch 1 and turn. (3 sts)

Row 11: Sk first ch, sc 3, change to black, ch 1 and turn. (3 sts)

Rows 12–13: Sk first ch, sc 3, ch 1 and turn. (3 sts)

Row 14: Sk first ch, sc 1, sk 1, sc 1. (2 sts)

- Fasten off, leaving a long tail for sewing.

RIGHT FRONT LEG

Row 1: With WS facing up, in orange work along the edge from the row 15 pm toward the row 11 pm. To rejoin beige yarn; (sl st 1, ch 1, sc 1) in row 15 pm st, sc 4 to row 11 pm st, ch 1 and turn. Remove these markers. (5 sts)

Row 2: Sk first ch, sc2tog, sc 3, ch 1 and turn. (4 sts)

Row 3: Sk first ch, sc2tog, sc 2, change to orange, ch 1 and turn. (3 sts)

Rows 4–10: Sk first ch, sc 3, ch 1 and turn. (3 sts)

Row 11: Sk first ch, sc 3, change to black, ch 1 and turn. (3 sts)

Rows 12–13: Sk first ch, sc 3, ch 1 and turn. (3 sts)

Row 14: Sk first ch, sc 1, sk 1, sc 1. (2 sts)

• Fasten off, leaving a long tail for sewing.

LEFT BACK LEG

Row 1: With RS facing up, in orange work along the edge from the row 24 pm toward the row 20 pm. To rejoin beige yarn; (sl st 1, ch 1, sc 1) in row 24 pm st, sc 4 to row 20 pm st, ch 1 and turn. Remove these markers. (5 sts)

Row 2: Sk first ch, sc2tog, sc 2, sc 2 in next st, ch 1 and turn. (5 sts)

Row 3: Sk first ch, sc 2 in next st, sc2tog twice, change to orange, ch 1 and turn. (4 sts)

Row 4: Sk first ch, sc2tog, sc 2, ch 1 and turn. (3 sts)

Rows 5–10: Sk first ch, sc 3, ch 1 and turn. (3 sts)

Row 11: Sk first ch, sc 3, change to black, ch 1 and turn. (3 sts)

Rows 12–13: Sk first ch, sc 3, ch 1 and turn. (3 sts)

Row 14: Sk first ch, sc 1, sk 1, sc 1. (2 sts)

• Fasten off, leaving a long tail for sewing.

RIGHT BACK LEG

Row 1: With WS facing up, work along the edge from the row 24 pm toward the row 20 pm. To rejoin beige yarn; (sl st 1, ch 1, sc 1) in row 24 pm st, sc 4 to row 20 pm st, ch 1 and turn. Remove these markers. (5 sts)

Row 2: Sk first ch, sc2tog, sc 2, sc 2 in next st, ch 1 and turn. (5 sts)

Row 3: Sk first ch, sc 2 in next st, sc2tog twice, change to orange, ch 1 and turn. (4 sts)

Row 4: Sk first ch, sc2tog, sc 2, ch 1 and turn. (3 sts)

Rows 5–10: Sk first ch, sc 3, ch 1 and turn. (3 sts)

Row 11: Sk first ch, sc 3, change to black, ch 1 and turn. (3 sts)

Rows 12–13: Sk first ch, sc 3, ch 1 and turn. (3 sts)

Row 14: Sk first ch, sc 1, sk 1, sc 1. (2 sts)

• Fasten off, leaving a long tail for sewing.

BACK STRIPE

• In reddish-orange, loosely ch 4 sts.

Row 1: Starting in second ch from hook, sc 3, ch 1 and turn. (3 sts)

Rows 2–3: Sk first ch, sc 3, ch 1 and turn. (3 sts)

Row 4: Sk first ch, sc 1, sc 2 in next st, sc 1, ch 1 and turn. (4 sts)

Rows 5–11: Sk first ch, sc 4, ch 1 and turn. (4 sts)

Row 12: Sk first ch, sc 1, sc2tog, sc 1, ch 1 and turn. (3 sts)

Rows 13–18: Sk first ch, sc 3, ch 1 and turn. (3 sts)

Row 19: Sk first ch, sc 1, sk 1, sc 1, ch 1 and turn. (2 sts)

Row 20: Sk first ch, sc2 in next st, sc 1, ch 1 and turn. (3 sts)

Row 21: Sk first ch, sc 1, sc2 in next st, sc 1, ch 1 and turn. (4 sts)

Row 22: Sk first ch, sc 1, sc2tog, sc 1, ch 1 and turn. (3 sts)

Row 23: Sk first ch, sc 1, sk 1, sc 1, ch 1 and turn. (2 sts)

Row 24: Sk first ch, sc2tog. (1 sts)

• Fasten off, leaving a long tail for sewing.

HEAD

• In reddish-orange, sc 8 in an adjustable ring.

Rnd 1: Sc 2 in each st around. (16 sts)

Rnd 2: *Sc 3, sc 2 in next st; rep from * 3 more times. (20 sts)

Rnd 3: *Sc 1, sc 2 in next st; rep from * 9 more times. (30 sts)

Rnd 4: *Sc 4, sc 2 in next st; rep from * 5 more times. (36 sts)

Rnds 5–6: Sc 36.

• Change to orange.

Rnd 7: Sc 14, change to reddish-orange, sc 3, hdc 2, sc 3, change to orange, sc 14. (36 sts)

Rnd 8: Sc 16, change to reddish-orange, sc 1, hdc 2, sc 1, change to orange, sc 16. (36 sts)

Rnd 9: *Sc 1, sc2tog; rep from * 5 more times, **sc2tog, sc 1; rep from ** 5 more times. (24 sts)

Rnd 10: Sc 24.

Rnd 11: *Sc 1, sc2tog; rep from * 7 more times. (16 sts)

Rnds 12–13: Sc 16.

• Stuff head.

Rnd 14: Sc2tog 8 times, ch 1 and turn. (8 sts)

Rnd 15: Sk first ch, sc 4. (4 sts)

• Fasten off, leaving a long tail for sewing.

MUZZLE

• In beige, sc 6 in an adjustable ring.

Rnd 1: *Sc 1, sc 2 in next st; rep from * 2 more times. (9 sts)

Rnds 2–3: Sc 9.

• Fasten off, leaving a long tail for sewing.

LIP

• In beige, sc 4 in an adjustable ring Do not join first st to last st. Ch 1 and turn.

Row 1: Sk first ch, sc 1, (sc 1, hdc 1) in next st, (hdc 1, sc 1) in next st, sc 1. (6 sts)

• Fasten off, leaving a long tail for sewing.

NOSE

• In black, sc 6 in an adjustable ring.

Rnd 1: Sc 6.

• Fasten off, fold circle in half, and secure edge with a whip stitch.

OUTSIDE EAR (MAKE 2)

• In reddish-orange, ch 5 and turn.

Rnd 1: Starting in second chain from hook and working in back ridge loops, sc 3, sc 3 in next st. Rotate chain so front loops are facing up. Starting in next st and working in front loops, sc 2, sc 2 in next st. (10 sts)

Rnd 2: Sc 2 in next st, sc 2, hdc 2 in next 3 sts, sc 2, sc 2 in next st, (sc 1, hdc 1, sc 1) in next st. (17 sts)

Rnd 3: Sc 4, hdc 2, hdc 2 in next 2 sts, hdc 2, sc 5, sc 3 in next st, sc 1. (21 sts)

Rnd 4: Sl st 3, change to beige, sl st 1, sc 2, sc 2 in next 4 sts, sc 2, change to reddish-orange, sl st 3, change to black, sl st 1, sc 2, sc 3 in next st, sc 2. (27 sts)

• Sl st in next st and fasten off. Weave in yarn tails.

INSIDE EAR (MAKE 2)

• In pink, loosely ch 5.

Rnd 1: Starting in second chain from hook and working in back ridge loops, sc 3, sc 3 in next st. Rotate chain so front loops are facing up. Starting in next st and working in front loops, sc 2, sc 2 in next st. (10 sts)

Rnd 2: Sc 2 in next st, sc 2, hdc 2 in next 3 sts, sc 2, sc 2 in next st, (sc 1, hdc 1, sc 1) in next st. (17 sts)

Rnd 3: Sc 4, hdc 2, hdc 2 in next 2 sts, hdc 2, sc 5, sc 3 in next st, sc 1. (21 sts)

• Fasten off, leaving a long tail for sewing.

BROW (MAKE 2)

• In reddish-orange, loosley ch 10.

Row 1: Starting in second ch from hook, sl st 9

• Fasten off, leaving a long tail for sewing.

ASSEMBLY

1. Attach the open edge of the muzzle to the front of the head with the row 15 flap overlapping the top of the muzzle. Stuff before closing the seam. Attach the back edge of the lip to the back of the muzzle. Sew the row 15 flap down onto the top of the muzzle. (Fig. A)

2. Place the WS of the pink inner ear against the RS of the outer ear. Using a tapestry needle and pink yarn, sew the pink inner ear to the inside surface of the outer ear. Pinch the beige sides of the outer ear together and secure with beige yarn. (Fig. B)

3. Sew the nose to the top front of the muzzle with the back sewn edge flush against the row 15 flap. Cut out 2 eye patches from beige felt, 2 eyes from white felt, 2 irises from reddish-orange felt, 2 pupils from black felt, and 2 eyelids from brown felt using templates. Assemble and glue or sew the eyes and eye patches together before gluing or sewing the eyes to the sides of the face. Sew the brows around the top half of the eye patches. Sew the ears to the head behind the eye patches with reddish-orange yarn. Cut out 4 to 5 4″ strands of reddish-orange yarn and attach as the forelock between the eye patches where the head changes color from reddish-orange to orange. Separate yarn plys with tapestry needle and trim. (Fig. C)

4. With the RS of the belly piece facing down, take one side piece and match up the legs to one side of the belly piece. With the leftover black yarn tails, first sew the edges of the black hooves together using a whip stitch, and secure. Using orange yarn and a

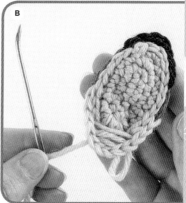

tapestry needle, start at the top corner of the neck and whip stitch the edges of the neck, chest, front leg, belly, back leg, and rump together (stopping before the tail). Tuck the yarn tails in as you sew. Tie off and repeat on the other side. (Fig. D)

5. Using the back of your crochet hook, push small amounts of stuffing down each leg until firm. Match up the edges of the back stripe to the side edges of the neck and back. Using reddish-orange yarn and a tapestry needle, whip stitch the edges together. Secure the reddish-orange tail top to the surface stitches of the beige-colored tail bottom and insert a bit of stuffing between the layers before closing the seam. Stuff the body through the neck hole. (Fig. E)

6. Sew the head to the open edge of the neck. Cut out 12 large spots and 4 small spots from beige felt using templates. Glue or sew spots to the sides of the body. (Fig. F)

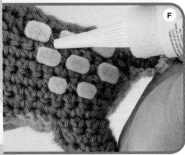

7. To keep legs from splaying out, attach beige yarn to the inside surface of one leg, pass yarn through to the inside surface of the opposite leg, then back again through the body to the starting point. Pull gently to draw the legs close to the body. (Fig. G)

LADY

Lady seems like the type of dog that would willingly take her bath just so she can look her best. With her long, silky ears and sweet, hopeful eyes, this little lady is one very pretty pooch.

WHAT YOU'LL NEED

- G/6 (4mm) crochet hook
- Worsted weight yarn in beige, tan, reddish-brown, and black
- Metal tapestry needle
- Felt in white, medium brown, dark brown, black, yellow, and aqua
- Fabric glue or needle and thread
- Stuffing

FINISHED SIZE: About 5.75" tall.

INSTRUCTIONS

MUZZLE

• In beige, sc 8 in an adjustable ring.
Rnd 1: Sc 2 in each st around. (16 sts)
Rnd 2: *Sc 7, sc 2 in next st; rep from *
1 more time. (18 sts)
Rnd 3: *Sc 4, sc2tog; rep from * 2 more
times. (15 sts)
Rnd 4: Sc 4, hdc 3, sc 3, hdc 3, sc 2.
(15 sts)

CREATE CENTER STRIPE

Rnd 5: Sl st 1, ch 9. Starting in second
ch from hook and working in back
ridge loops; hdc 2, dc 3, hdc 3, sl st 1 in
the next st of rnd 4.
• Fasten off, leaving a long tail for
  sewing.

HEAD

• In tan, sc 6 in an adjustable ring.
Rnd 1: Sc 2 in each st around. (12 sts)
Rnd 2: *Sc 1, sc 2 in next st; rep from *
5 more times. (18 sts)
Rnd 3: *Sc 5, sc 2 in next st; rep from *
2 more times. (21 sts)
Rnd 4: *Sc 6, sc 2 in next st; rep from *
2 more times. (24 sts)
Rnd 5: *Sc 5, sc 2 in next st; rep from *
3 more times. (28 sts)
Rnd 6: *Sc 6, sc 2 in next st; rep from *
3 more times. (32 sts)
Rnds 7-8: Sc 8, hdc 16, sc 8. (32 sts)
Rnd 9: Sc2tog 4 times, sc 16, sc2tog 4
times. (24 sts)
Rnd 10: *Sc 1, sc2tog; rep from * 7
more times. (16 sts)
Rnd 11: *Sc 2, sc2tog; rep from * 3
more times. (12 sts)
• Stuff head.
Rnd 12: Sc2tog 6 times. (6 sts)
• Fasten off, leaving a long tail for
  sewing.

CHIN

• In beige, sc 5 in an adjustable ring.
Rnd 1: Sc 2 in each st around. (10 sts)
Rnd 2: *Sc 1, sc 2 in next st: rep from *
4 more times. (15 sts)
Rnd 3: Sc2tog 2 times, pm, sc2tog 2
times, sl st 7. (11 sts)
• Do not stuff. Fasten off, leaving a
  long tail for sewing.

NOSE

• In black, sc 5 in an adjustable ring.
Rnd 1: Sl st 1, sc 3 in next st, sl st 2, sc 3
in next st. (9 sts)
Rnd 2: In blo; sl st 4, sc2tog, pm, sl st
3. (8 sts)
• Fasten off, leaving a long tail for
  sewing.

EAR (MAKE 2)

• In reddish-brown, loosely ch 4 and
  turn.
Row 1: Starting second ch from hook,
sc 1, sc 2 in next 1 st, sc 1, ch 1 and turn.
(4 sts)
Row 2: Sk first ch, sc 1, sc 2 in next 2
sts, sc 1, ch 1 and turn. (6 sts)
Rows 3-8: Sk first ch, sc 6, ch 1 and
turn. (6 sts)
Row 9: Sk first ch, sc 2, sc 2 in next 2
sts, sc 2, ch 1 and turn. (8 sts)
Rows 10-12: Sk first ch, sc 8, ch 1 and
turn. (8 sts)
Row 13: Sk first ch, sc 1, hdc 2, dc 2,
hdc 2, sc 1, ch 1 and turn. (8 sts)
Row 14: Sk first ch, sc2tog, hdc 4,
sc2tog. (6 sts)
• Fasten off, leaving a long tail for
  sewing.

BODY

• In tan, sc 10 in an adjustable ring.
Rnd 1: Sc 2 in each st around. (20 sts)
Rnd 2: Sc 20.
Rnd 3: *Sc 3, sc 2 in next st; rep from *
4 more times. (25 sts)

Rnds 4–6: Sc 25.

Rnd 7: *Sc 3, sc2tog; rep from * 4 more times. (20 sts)

Rnds 8–11: Sc 20.

Rnd 12: *Sc 4, sc 2 in next st; rep from * 3 more times. (24 sts)

Rnds 13–15: Sc 24.

Rnd 16: *Sc 2, sc2tog; rep from * 5 more times. (18 sts)

Rnds 17–18: Sc 18.

Rnd 19: *Sc 1, sc2tog; rep from * 5 more times. (12 sts)

• Stuff body.

Rnd 20: Sc2tog 6 times. (6 sts)

• Fasten off and close hole at the front of the body.

BELLY

• In beige, loosely ch 10.

Rnd 1: Starting in second chain from hook and working in back ridge loops, sc 8, sc 3 in next st. Rotate chain so front loops are facing up. Starting in next st and working in front loops, sc 7, sc 2 in next st. (20 sts)

Rnd 2: Sc 2 in next st, sc 5, hdc 2, hdc 2 in next 3 sts, hdc 2, sc 5, sc 2 in next 2 st. (26 sts)

Rnd 3: Sl st 7, hdc 2, hdc 2 in next 6 sts, hdc 2, sl st 9. (32 sts)

• Fasten off, leaving a long tail for sewing.

NECK

• In tan, loosely ch 16 and join last chain to first chain with a slip stitch to form a ring.

Rnd 1: Sc 16.

Rnd 2: *Sc 2, sc2tog; rep from * 3 more times. (12 sts)

Rnd 3: Sc 12.

Rnd 4: *Sc 2, sc 2 in next st; rep from * 3 more times. (16 sts)

• Fasten off, leaving a long tail for sewing.

LEG (MAKE 4)

• In beige, sc 6 in an adjustable ring.

Rnd 1: Sc 1, sc 2 in next st, hdc 2 in next 2 sts, sc 2 in next st, sc 1. (10 sts)

Rnd 2: Sc 2, hdc 6, sc 2. (10 sts)

Rnd 3: Sc 3, sc2tog 2 times, sc 3. (8 sts)

• Change to tan.

Rnd 4: In flo; *sc 1, sc 2 in next st; rep from * 3 more times. (12 sts)

Rnds 5–7: Sc 12.

Rnd 8: *Sc 2, sc 2 in next st; rep from * 3 more times. (16 sts)

Rnd 9: Sc 16.

Rnd 10: *Sc 2, sc2tog; rep from * 3 more times. (12 sts)

• Stuff leg.

Rnd 11: Sc2tog 6 times. (6 sts)

• Fasten off, flatten seam, and sew closed.

TAIL

• In tan, sc 4 in an adjustable ring.

Rnd 1: Sc 4.

Rnd 2: Sc 2 in next st, sc 3. (5 sts)

Rnd 3: Sc 2 in next st, sc 4. (6 sts)

• Stuff tail.

Rnd 4: *Sc2tog, sc 1; rep from * 1 more time. (4 sts)

• Fasten off, leaving a long tail for sewing.

ASSEMBLY

1. With the last rnd of the head facing the back, attach the open end of the muzzle to the front of the head and stuff before closing the seam. Sew the stripe above the muzzle down to the front of the head. Attach the open edge of the nose to the front of the muzzle (place marker will indicate the bottom of the nose). Using beige yarn, loop a long stitch through the front of the muzzle (directly below the nose and into the roof of the mouth 2 to 3 times, pulling tightly to form the lip cleft. (Fig. A)

2. Cut 8 to 10 7" pieces and attach as a fringe to the top edge of the ear. Using a tapestry needle, separate the yarn plys. (Fig. B) Apply a light coating of fabric glue to the outside surface of the ear and gently press the separated plys against the glue. Trim the end of the fringe to match the edge of the ear shape.

3. Flatten and sew the open edge of the chin to the head at the back of the muzzle (do not stuff). To shape the lower lip, sew 2 to 3 running stitches through the bottom of the chin, into the muzzle, and back out through the chin. Using black yarn and a tapestry needle, apply long stitches along the crease of the mouth where the chin meets the muzzle, roughly 1 row back from the front, pulling firmly. (Fig. C)

4. Cut out 2 eyelids from dark brown felt, 2 eyes from white felt, 2 irises from medium brown felt, and 2 pupils and 2 eyelashes from black felt using templates. Assemble and glue or sew the eyes together before gluing or sewing them to the front of the face on either side of the face stripe. Attach the ears to the sides of the head. Using black yarn and a tapestry needle, apply long stitches and overcast stitches above the eyes to create eyebrows. (Fig. D)

5. Using black yarn, form the toes by looping a long stitch 1 to 2 times through the front of the feet in 2 different locations. (Fig. E–page 72)

6. With the last rnd of the body facing forward, sew one edge of the neck to

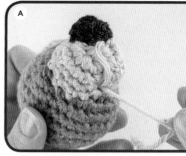

the top of the body at the front. Sew the head to the open edge at the top of the neck and stuff the neck before closing the seam. Cut out 1 dog tag from yellow felt using template. Cut a $3/4$" wide by 3" long strip of aqua felt. Fold the long way and glue or sew the long edges together. Glue or sew the medal to the front of the collar. Wrap the collar around the neck and sew the short ends together. (Fig. F)

7. Using beige yarn and a running stitch, attach the belly piece to the chest and belly of body with the larger end of the belly piece at the chest. Sew the tail to the back of the body and sew the closed edges of the legs to the body at the shoulders and hips. (Fig. G)

8. To keep legs from splaying out, attach tan yarn to the inside surface of one leg, pass yarn through the body to the inside surface of the opposite leg, then back again through the body to the starting point. Pull gently to draw the legs close to the body. (Fig. H)

PINOCCHIO

"I got no strings" would certainly be a bit of a fib for a crocheted Pinocchio made entirely of yarn. You can make Pinocchio's nose as long as you like, depending on how honest your version happens to be!

WHAT YOU'LL NEED

- G/6 (4mm) crochet hook
- Worsted weight yarn in dark yellow, black, beige, rosy beige, white, medium blue, light yellow, and dark brown
- Metal tapestry needle
- Felt in white, black, yellow, red, and medium blue
- Fabric glue or needle and thread
- Stuffing

FINISHED SIZE: About 10" tall.

INSTRUCTIONS

HEAD

• In beige, sc 8 in an adjustable ring.
Rnd 1: Sc 2 in each st around. (16 sts)
Rnd 2: *Sc 3, sc 2 in next st; rep from *
3 more times. (20 sts)
Rnd 3: *Sc 1, sc 2 in next st; rep from *
9 more times. (30 sts)
Rnd 4: *Sc 4, sc 2 in next st; rep from *
5 more times. (36 sts)
Rnds 5-7: Sc 36.
Rnd 8: *Sc 1, sc2tog; rep from * 11 more
times. (24 sts)
Rnd 9: Sc2tog 3 times, hdc 1, hdc 2 in
next 3 sts, sc 4, hdc 2 in next 3 sts, hdc
1, sc2tog 3 times. (24 sts)
Rnd 10: Sc 6, hdc 3, sc 1, sc2tog, pm,
sc2tog, sc 1, hdc 3, sc 6. (22 sts)
Rnd 11: Sc2tog, sc 18, sc2tog. (20 sts)
Rnd 12: *Sc 3, sc2tog; rep from * 3
more times. (16 sts)
• Stuff head.
Rnd 13: Sc2tog 8 times. (8 sts)
Rnds 14-15: Sc 8.
• Stuff neck.
• Fasten off, leaving a long tail for
sewing.

NOSE

• In rosy beige, sc 5 in an adjustable
ring.
Rnds 1-3: Sc 5.
• Fasten off.
TIP: *If your Pinocchio happens to be a
big fibber, you can add more rows to
your nose!*

BODY

• In red, sc 10 in an adjustable ring.
Rnd 1: Sc 2 in each st around. (20 sts)
Rnd 2: Sc 20.
Rnd 3: *Sc 3, sc 2 in next st; rep from *
4 more times. (25 sts)
Rnds 4-6: Sc 25.
• Change to light yellow.

Rnd 7: In blo; *sc 3, sc2tog in next sc;
rep from * 4 more times. (20 sts)
Rnds 8-9: Sc 20.
Rnd 10: *Sc 3, sc2tog; rep from * 3
more times. (16 sts)
Rnd 11: Sc 16.
• Stuff body.
Rnd 12: Sc2tog 8 times. (8 sts)
• Fasten off, leaving a long tail for
sewing.

LEG (MAKE 2)

• In beige, sc 6 in an adjustable ring.
Rnds 1-4: Sc 6.
• Change to red.
Rnd 5: In flo; sc 2 in each st around.
(12 sts)
Rnd 6: In blo; sc 12. (12 sts)
• Fasten off, leaving a long tail for
sewing. Stuff legs.

EAR (MAKE 2)

• In beige, sc 6 in an adjustable ring.
Do not join first st to last st. Ch 1 and
turn.
Row 1: Sl st 6.
• Fasten off, leaving a long tail for
sewing.

HAND (MAKE 2)

• In white, sc 6 in an adjustable ring.
Rnd 1: Sc 2 in each st around. (12 sts)
Rnds 2-3: Sc 12.
Rnd 4: *Sc 1, sc2tog; rep from * 3 more
times. (8 sts)
• Stuff hand.
Rnd 5: Sc2tog 4 times. (4 sts)
Rnd 6: In flo; sc 2 in each st around.
(8 sts)
• Fasten off, leaving a long tail for
sewing.

FINGERS (MAKE 8)

• In white, sc 6 in an adjustable ring.
Rnd 1: Sc 6.
• Fasten off, leaving a long tail for
sewing. Do not stuff.

ARM (MAKE 2)

• In beige, sc 6 in an adjustable ring.
Rnds 1–2: Sc 6.
• Change to light yellow.
Rnd 3: In flo; sc 2 in each st around. (12 sts)
Rnd 4: In blo; sc 12.
Rnd 5: Sc 12.
Rnd 6: Sc2tog 6 times. (6 sts)
• Stuff arm. Flatten seam and sew closed, leaving a long tail for sewing.

SHOE (MAKE 2)

• In brown, sc 8 in an adjustable ring.
Rnd 1: Sc 2 in each st around. (16 sts)
Rnd 2: Sc 16.
Rnd 3: *Sc 7, sc 2 in next st; rep from * 1 more time. (18 sts)
Rnd 4: *Sc 7, sc2tog in next sc; rep from * 1 more time. (16 sts)
Rnd 5: *Sc 2, sc2tog; rep from * 3 more times. (12 sts)
Rnds 6–8: Sc 12.
• Stuff.
Rnd 9: Sc2tog 6 times. (6 sts)
• Fasten off and close hole in back of shoe.

FOOT TOP (MAKE 2)

• In beige, sc 6 in an adjustable ring. Fasten off, but do not join first and last stitches of the ring in order to retain a semicircle shape.

SHOE STRAP (MAKE 2)

• In brown, loosely ch 7.
Row 1: Starting in second ch from hook, sl st 6. (6 sts)
• Fasten off, leaving a long tail for sewing.

BOW TIE

• In medium blue, loosely ch 12 and join last chain to first chain with a slip stitch to form a ring.
Rnds 1–3: Sc 12.
• Fasten off, leaving a long tail for sewing.

COLLAR

• In white, loosely ch 9.
Row 1: Starting in second ch from hook, sc 2 in next 8 sts, ch 1 and turn. (16 sts)
Row 2: Sk first st, *sc 1, sc 2 in next st; rep from * 7 more times, ch 1 and turn. (24 sts)
Row 3: Sk first st, sc 24.
• Fasten off, leaving a long tail for sewing.

SUSPENDERS (MAKE 2)

• In red, loosely ch 18.
Row 1: Starting in second ch from hook, sc 3 in next st, sc 16. (19 sts)
• Fasten off, leaving a long tail for sewing.

VEST

• In black, sc 8 in an adjustable ring.
Rnd 1: *Sc 1, sc 3 in next st; rep from * 3 more times. (16 sts)
Rnd 2: Sc 2, *sc 3 in next st, sc 3; rep from * 2 more times, sc 3 in next st, sc 1. (24 sts)
Rnd 3: Sc 3, sc 3 in next st, sc 5, (sc 2, pm, sc 1) in next st, sc 5, sc 3 in next st, sc 5, (sc 2, pm, sc 1) in next st, sc 2. (32 sts)
Rnd 4: Sl st 4, sc 2 in next st, ch 8, skip ahead and sc 2 in next pm st, sc 7, sc 2 in next st, ch 8, skip ahead and sc 2 in the next pm st, sl st 3. Remove marker. (38 sts)
Rnd 5: Sl st 6, sc 8 in ch sp, hdc 3 in next st, sc 9, hdc 3 in next st, sc 8 in ch sp, sl st 5. (42 sts)
• Change to white.
Rnd 6: Sc 42.
• Fasten off, leaving a long tail for sewing.

HAIR

• In black, sc 8 in an adjustable ring.
Rnd 1: Sc 2 in each st around. (16 sts)
Rnd 2: *Sc 3, sc 2 in next st; rep from *

3 more times. (20 sts)

Rnd 3: *Sc 1, sc 2 in next st; rep from * 9 more times. (30 sts)

Rnd 4: *Sc 4, sc 2 in next st; rep from * 5 more times. (36 sts)

Rnds 5–7: Sc 36.

Rnd 8: Sc 3, sc 3 in next st, sc2tog 2 times, sl st 3, (sc 1, hdc 2) in next st, sl st 2, hdc 2 in next st, (hdc 1, dc 1) in next st, dc 2 in next st, (dc 1, tr 2, dc 1) in next st, dc 2 in next st, (dc 1, hdc 1) in next st, hdc 2 in next st, sl st 2, (hdc 2, sc 1) in next st, sl st 3, sc2tog 2 times, sc 3 in next st, sc 4. (49 sts)

• Fasten off, leaving a long tail for sewing.

HAT

• In dark yellow, sc 6 in an adjustable ring.

Rnd 1: *Sc 2, sc 2 in next st; rep from * 1 more time. (8 sts)

Rnd 2: *Sc 1, sc 2 in next st; rep from * 3 more times. (12 sts)

Rnd 3: *Sc 2, sc 2 in next st; rep from * 3 more times. (16 sts)

Rnd 4: Sc 16.

Rnd 5: *Sc 3, sc 2 in next st; rep from * 3 more times. (20 sts)

Rnd 6: *Sc 1, sc 2 in next st; rep from * 9 more times. (30 sts)

Rnd 7: Sc 30.

Rnd 8: *Sc 4, sc 2 in next st; rep from * 5 more times. (36 sts)

Rnd 9: Sc 36.

Rnd 10: In flo; hdc 10, sc 16, hdc 10. (36 sts)

Rnd 11: *Hdc 1, hdc 2 in next st; rep from * 4 more times. **Sc 1, sc 2 in next st; rep from ** 7 more times, ***hdc 1, hdc 2 in next st; rep from *** 4 more times. (54 sts)

• Fasten off, leaving a long tail for sewing.

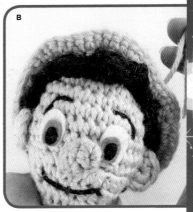

ASSEMBLY

1. Locate the marker at the front of the head and attach the open edge of the nose. Using black yarn and a tapestry needle, secure the hair to the head using a running stitch, taking care to leave the double and triple crochet stitches at the front of the head loose. Sew the ears to the sides of the head. (Fig. A–page 77)

2. Cut out 2 eyes from white felt, 2 irises from medium blue felt, and 2 pupils from black felt using templates. Assemble and glue or sew the eyes together before gluing or sewing them to the front of the face. Using black yarn and a tapestry needle, apply long stitches and overcast stitches to the face to create a mouth and eyebrows. With the fastened-off yarn tail positioned at the back, secure rnd 10 of the hat to the head using a running stitch to create a hat brim. Stuff the hat before closing seam. (Fig. B–page 77)

3. Cut out 1 feather from red felt using template. Cut a $1/4$"-wide strip of medium blue felt long enough to wrap around the center of the hat. Slip the bottom of the red feather behind the hat band on the left side of the hat and sew or glue the band and feather in place. (Fig. C–page 77)

4. Sew the open ends of the fingers to the ends of the hands. Using black yarn, add 3 short stitches to the back of the hands.

5. With the larger end of the shoe at the front, sew the bottom of the leg onto the top of the shoe and sew the foot top to the top of the shoe and the front edge of the leg. Sew the shoe strap over the foot top. (Fig. D)

6. Flatten the bow tie piece and wrap the tail tightly around the center to form the two sides of the bow tie and secure. (Fig. E–page 78)

7. Attach the head to the open end of the body. Using white yarn, sew the hands to the ends of the arms. Attach the arms to the shoulders. Drape the suspenders over the shoulders and secure at the front and back of the body. Slip the vest over the shoulders and suspenders and secure with a few stitches in the back. Wrap the collar around the neck with the opening in the front and sew in place. Sew the bow tie to the front of the neck between the edges of the collar. (Fig. F–page 78)

8. Cut out 2 buttons from yellow felt using template. Glue or sew the buttons to the front ends of the suspenders.

9. Attach the open ends of the legs to the bottom of the body. Add more stuffing if needed before closing the seam. With medium blue yarn and a tapestry needle, sew a pattern of lines and Xs onto the sides of the pant legs, using short stitches and back stitches. (Fig. G–page 78)

JIMINY CRICKET

Jiminy not only looks dapper with his top hat and umbrella—
he is the perfect size to ride along in a book bag or purse.
Now there's no excuse to ever be without your own personal
conscience.

WHAT YOU'LL NEED

- G/6 (4mm) crochet hook
- Worsted weight yarn in green, medium blue, white, yellow, royal purple, khaki, dark blue, dusty rose, and black
- Metal tapestry needle
- White, black, light pink, and orange felt
- Fabric glue or needle and thread
- Stuffing

FINISHED SIZE: About 9" tall.

INSTRUCTIONS

HEAD

• In green, sc 8 in an adjustable ring.
Rnd 1: Sc 2 in each st around. (16 sts)
Rnd 2: Sc 16.
Rnd 3: *Sc 3, sc 2 in next st; rep from * 3 more times. (20 sts)
Rnd 4: Sc 20.
Rnd 5: *Sc 1, sc 2 in next st; rep from * 9 more times. (30 sts)
Rnd 6: Sc 30.
Rnd 7: *Sc 4, sc 2 in next st; rep from * 5 more times. (36 sts)
Rnd 8: *Sc 1, sc2tog; rep from * 11 more times. (24 sts)
Rnd 9: Sc 5, hdc 1, hdc 2 in next 3 sts, hdc 1, sc 4, hdc 1, hdc 2 in next 3 sts, hdc 1, sc 5. (30 sts)
Rnd 10: Sc2tog 3 times, hdc 5, sc 4, pm, sc 4, hdc 5, sc2tog 3 times. (24 sts)
Rnd 11: Sc 4, sc2tog 2 times, sc 8, sc2tog 2 times, sc 4. (20 sts)
Rnd 12: *Sc 3, sc2tog; rep from * 3 more times. (16 sts)
• Stuff head.
Rnd 13: Sc2tog 8 times. (8 sts)
• Fasten off, leaving a long tail.

BODY

• In khaki, sc 10 in an adjustable ring.
Rnd 1: Sc 2 in each st around. (20 sts)
Rnd 2: Sc 20.
Rnd 3: *Sc 3, sc 2 in next st; rep from * 4 more times. (25 sts)
Rnds 4–5: Sc 25.
• Change to dusty rose.
Rnd 6: In blo; sc 25.
Rnd 7: *Sc 3, sc2tog in next sc; rep from * 4 more times. (20 sts)
Rnd 8: Sc 20.
Rnd 9: Sc 11, change to yellow, in blo; hdc 3 in next st, change to dusty rose, tbl; sc 8. (22 sts)

Rnd 10: *Sc 3, sc2tog; rep from * 1 more time, sc 1, change to yellow, hdc 2 in next 3 hdc, change to dusty rose, sc 1, sc2tog, sc 3, sc2tog. (21 sts)
• Stuff body.
Rnd 11: Sc2tog 4 times, sc 1, change to yellow, sk 2, sl st 1, sk 2, change to dusty rose, sc 1, sc2tog 3 times. (10 sts)
Tip: *Shirt collar is worked in the dusty rose stitches only.*
Row 12: Sl st 5, change to white, ch 1 and turn.
Row 13: Sk first ch, sc 8, ch 1 and turn. (8 sts)
Row 14: Sk first ch, sc 2 in next st, sc 6, sc 2 in next st, ch 1 and turn. (10 sts)
Row 15: Sk first ch, sc 2 in next st, sc 8, sc 2 in next st, ch 1 and turn. (12 sts)
Row 16: Sk first ch, sc 2 in next st, sc 10, sc 2 in next st, ch 1 and turn. (14 sts)
Row 17: Sk first ch, sl st 14.
• Fasten off, leaving a long tail.

HAND AND ARM (MAKE 2)

• In white, sc 6 in an adjustable ring.
Rnd 1: Sc 2 in each st around. (12 sts)
Rnds 2–3: Sc 12.
Rnd 4: *Sc 1, sc2tog; rep from * 3 more times. (8 sts)
• Stuff hand.
Rnd 5: Sc2tog 4 times. (4 sts)
• Change to black.
Rnd 6: In flo; sc 2 in each st around. (8 sts)
Rnds 7–8: Sc 8.
Rnd 9: *Sc 2, sc2tog; rep from * 1 more time. (6 sts)
• Stuff arm. Flatten seam and sew closed, leaving a long tail for sewing.

FINGERS (MAKE 8)

• In white, sc 6 in an adjustable ring.
Rnd 1: Sc 6.
• Fasten off, leaving a long tail for sewing. Do not stuff.

LEG (MAKE 2)

• In khaki, sc 6 in an adjustable ring.

Rnd 1: In blo; sc 6.

Rnd 2: Sc 6.

Rnd 3: *Sc 2, sc 2 in next st; rep from * 1 more time. (8 sts)

Rnds 4–5: Sc 8.

• Fasten off, leaving a long tail for sewing. Stuff leg.

SHOE (MAKE 2)

• In dark blue, sc 8 in an adjustable ring.

Rnd 1: Sc 2 in each st around. (16 sts)

Rnd 2: Sc 16.

Rnd 3: *Sc 7, sc 2 in next st; rep from * 1 more time. (18 sts)

Rnd 4: *Sc 7, sc2tog; rep from * 1 more time. (16 sts)

Rnd 5: *Sc 2, sc2tog; rep from * 3 more times. (12 sts)

Rnds 6–8: Sc 12.

• Stuff shoe.

Rnd 9: Sc2tog 6 times. (6 sts)

• Fasten off and close hole in back of shoe.

SPAT (MAKE 2)

• In yellow, make a slip knot with a 10″ to 12″ tail and loosely ch 15. Join last chain to first chain with a slip stitch to form a ring.

Rnd 1: Sc 15.

Rnd 2: *Sc 3, sc2tog; rep from * 2 more times. (12 sts)

Rnd 3: *Sc 2, sc2tog; rep from * 2 more times. (9 sts)

Rnd 4: In flo; sl st 9.

• Fasten off, leaving a long tail for sewing. Reusing the long yarn tail at the beg slip knot, sl st 1 in the st at the base of the slip knot, ch 8, and fasten off.

JACKET

• In black, sc 8 in an adjustable ring.

Rnd 1: *Sc 1, sc 3 in next st; rep from * 3 more times. (16 sts)

Rnd 2: Sc 2, *sc 3 in next st, sc 3: rep from * 2 more times, sc 3 in next st, sc 1. (24 sts)

Rnd 3: Sc 3, sc 3 in next st, sc 1, hdc 3, sc 1, sc 3 in next st, (sc 1, hdc 1, dc 1) in next st, (dc 1, hdc 1, sl st 1) in next st, sk 1, (sl st 1, hdc 1, dc 1) in next st, (dc 1, hdc 1, sc 1) in next st, sc 3 in next st, sc 1, hdc 3, sc 1, sc 3 in next st, sc 2. (39 sts)

Rnd 4: Sl st 4, hdc 3 in next st, hdc 2, dc 3, hdc 2, sc 3 in next st, sl st 2, hdc 1, dc 2 in next st, (hdc 1, sl st 1) in next st, sl st 4, (sl st 1, hdc 1) in next st, dc 2 in next st, hdc 1, sl st 2, sc 3 in next st, hdc 2, dc 3, hdc 2, hdc 3 in next st, sl st 3. (51 sts)

Rnd 5: In flo; sc 4, tbl; hdc 1, hdc 3 in next st, hdc 1, sc 1, (hdc 1, dc 1, hdc 1) in next st, sk 1, sl st 10, sc 3 in next st, sl st 1, sc 3 in next st, sl st 6, sc 3 in next st, sl st 1, sc 3 in next st, sl st 10, sk 1, (hdc 1, dc 1, hdc 1) in next st, sc 1, hdc 1, hdc 3 in next st, hdc 1, in flo; sc 3. (65 sts)

• Fasten off, leaving a long tail for sewing.

TOP HAT

• In medium blue, sc 8 in an adjustable ring.

Rnd 1: Sc 2 in each st around. (16 sts)

Rnd 2: *Sc 1, sc 2 in next st; rep from * 7 more times. (24 sts)

Rnd 3: *Sc 2, sc 2 in next st; rep from * 7 more times. (32 sts)

Rnd 4: *Sc 3, sc 2 in next st; rep from * 7 more times. (40 sts)

Rnd 5: In blo; *sc 3, sc2tog in next st; rep from * 7 more times. (32 sts)

Rnd 6: Sc 32.

Rnd 7: *Sc 2, sc2tog in next st; rep from * 7 more times. (24 sts)

Rnd 8: Sc 24.

Rnd 9: *Sc 1, sc2tog in next st; rep from * 7 more times. (16 sts)

Rnd 10: *Sc 3, sc 2 in next st; rep from * 3 more times. (20 sts)

Rnd 11: *Sc 4, sc 2 in next st; rep from *
3 more times. (24 sts)
Rnd 12: In flo; *sc 1, sc 2 in next st; rep
from * 11 more times. (36 sts)
Rnd 13: Hdc 15, dc 3 in next st, sl st 4,
dc 3 in next st, hdc 15. (40 sts)
• Fasten off, leaving a long tail for
  sewing.

UMBRELLA

• In royal purple, sc 4 in an adjustable
  ring.
Rnd 1: *Sc 1, sc 2 in next st; rep from * 1
more time. (6 sts)
Rnd 2: *Sc 2, sc 2 in next st; rep from *
1 more time. (8 sts)
Rnds 3–4: Sc 8.
Rnd 5: *Sc 2, sc2tog; rep from * 1 more
time. (6 sts)
Rnd 6: Sc 6.
• Stuff lightly.
Rnd 7: *Sc 1, sc2tog; rep from * 1 more
time. (4 sts)
Rnd 8: In flo; hdc 2 in each st around.
(8 sts)
• Fasten off, leaving a long tail for
  sewing.

UMBRELLA HANDLE

• In yellow, make a slip knot with a 6″
  tail and loosely ch 5.
Row 1: Starting in second ch from
hook and working in back ridge loops,
(hdc 2, sc 1) in next st, sc 3. (6 sts)
• Fasten off, leaving a long tail for
  sewing.

ASSEMBLY

1. To construct the umbrella, thread
both yarn tails on the umbrella handle
onto a tapestry needle and draw them
up through the umbrella from the
rnd 7 to rnd 1 so that the base of the
handle is flush against rnd 7 of the
umbrella. Tie a double square knot
with the two yarn tails at the top of

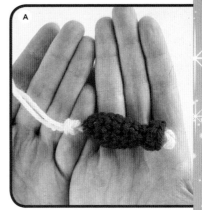

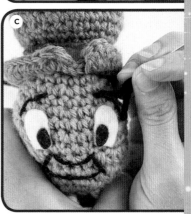

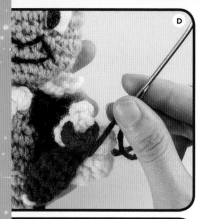

the umbrella to make a point. Fasten off the yarn and work the tails in. (Fig. A–page 83)

2. Pin and sew the top and sides of the jacket to the back half of the body, taking care to keep the white collar free. (Fig. B–page 83)

3. Cut out 2 eyes from white felt and 2 pupils from black felt using templates. Assemble and glue or sew the eyes together before gluing or sewing the eyes to the front of the face (indicated by place marker). Stuff and sew the opening of the hat to the top of the head (taking care to leave the hat brim free). Cut a $1/4$"-wide strip of orange felt long enough to wrap around the hat and sew or glue in place. Using black yarn and a tapestry needle, apply short and long stitches to the face for the nose, mouth, and eyebrows. (Fig. C–page 83)

4. Sew the open ends of the fingers to the ends of the hands. Using the leftover black yarn tail, sew 3 short stitches on the back of the hands before fastening off the yarn and weaving in the ends.

5. Sew the open the end of the head to the open end of the body. Cut out 1 button from light pink felt using template and glue or sew to the front of the vest. Sew the arms to the body at the shoulders. Sew the umbrella to the inside of the fingers on Jiminy's left hand. (Fig. D)

6. With the larger end of the foot facing forward, sew the first rnd of the leg to the top of the foot at the ankle. Slip the yellow piece over the top of the leg and draw the ch-8 yellow strap under the foot to the other side of the yellow piece and sew in place. Weave in the yarn tail at the top of the yellow piece. (Fig. E)

7. Stuff the leg and sew the open end to the bottom of the body. (Fig. F)

TEMPLATES

If you choose to work the patterns using a different yarn and/or hook size than indicated, be sure to resize your templates accordingly.

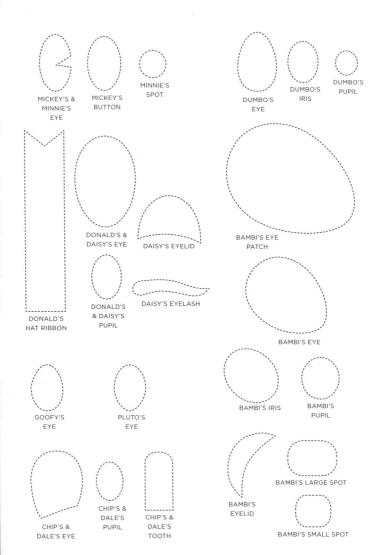

MICKEY'S & MINNIE'S EYE

MICKEY'S BUTTON

MINNIE'S SPOT

DUMBO'S EYE

DUMBO'S IRIS

DUMBO'S PUPIL

DONALD'S & DAISY'S EYE

DAISY'S EYELID

BAMBI'S EYE PATCH

DONALD'S HAT RIBBON

DONALD'S & DAISY'S PUPIL

DAISY'S EYELASH

BAMBI'S EYE

GOOFY'S EYE

PLUTO'S EYE

BAMBI'S IRIS

BAMBI'S PUPIL

CHIP'S & DALE'S EYE

CHIP'S & DALE'S PUPIL

CHIP'S & DALE'S TOOTH

BAMBI'S EYELID

BAMBI'S LARGE SPOT

BAMBI'S SMALL SPOT

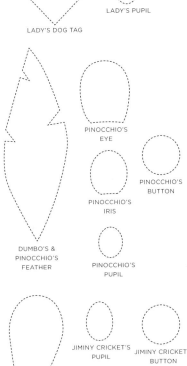

LADY'S EYELASH

LADY'S EYELID

LADY'S EYE

LADY'S IRIS

LADY'S PUPIL

LADY'S DOG TAG

PINOCCHIO'S EYE

PINOCCHIO'S IRIS

PINOCCHIO'S BUTTON

DUMBO'S & PINOCCHIO'S FEATHER

PINOCCHIO'S PUPIL

JIMINY CRICKET'S EYE

JIMINY CRICKET'S PUPIL

JIMINY CRICKET'S BUTTON

ASSEMBLED EYES

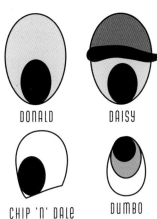

DONALD

DAISY

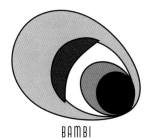

CHIP 'N' DALE

DUMBO

BAMBI

LADY

PINOCCHIO

JIMINY CRICKET

ABBREVIATIONS

( )	Work instructions within parentheses as many times as directed.
*	Repeat instructions following the asterisk(s) as directed.
"	inch(es)
alt	alternate
approx	approximately
beg	begin(ning)
bet	between
blo	back loop only
ch	chain
ch sp	chain space
cont	continue(ing)
dc	double crochet
flo	front loop only
hdc	half double crochet
lp(s)	loop(s)
m	meter(s)
mm	millimeter(s)
oz	ounce(s)
pm	place marker
prev	previous
rem	remaining
rep	repeat(s)
rnd(s)	round(s)
RS	right side
sc	single crochet
sc2tog	single crochet 2 together
sk	skip
sl	slip stitch
sp	space
st(s)	stitch(es)
tog	together
tr	triple crochet
tbl	through both loops
WS	wrong side
yd(s)	yard(s)
YO	yarn over

CROCHET HOOK SIZES AND CONVERSIONS

METRIC SIZES(mm)	US SIZES	UK/CANADIAN
2.0	-	14
2.25	B/1	13
2.5	-	12
2.75	C/2	-
3.0	-	11
3.25	D/3	10
3.5	E/4	9
3.75	F/5	-
4.0	G/6	8
4.5	7	7
5.0	H/8	6
5.5	I/9	5
6.0	J/10	4
6.5	K/10 1/2	3
7.0	-	2
8.0	L/11	0
9.0	M/13	00
10.0	N/15	000

YARN WEIGHTS

	SUPER FINE (1)	FINE (2)	LIGHT (3)	MEDIUM (4)	BULKY (5)
TYPE OF YARN	SOCK	SPORT	DK	WORSTED	CHUNKY
	FINGERING	BABY	LIGHT	AFGHAN	CRAFT
	BABY		WORSTED	ARAN	RUG
CROCHET GAUGE	21–32 STS	16–20 STS	12–17 STS	11–14 STS	8–11 STS
RECOMMENDED U.S. HOOK SIZE	B-1 TO E-4	E-4 TO 7	7 TO I-9	I-9 TO K-10 1/2	K-10 1/2 TO M-13

DEDICATION

For Mitchell, whose memory inspires me to cherish the magical moments of life with my family everyday.

ACKNOWLEDGMENTS

A big thank you to Nicole and the folks over at becker&mayer! Book Producers for allowing me the opportunity to be a part of a brand that I have treasured since I was very little.

Thank you also to my yarn donors over at Knit Picks, Berroco, and Cascade for being so speedy and generous with their material donations for this book.

And thank you to my husband who puts up with the seemingly endless amount of yarn in our home and my children who have been kind enough to not hide, eat, trash, flush, sully, or unravel the various projects I happen to leave lying about.

ABOUT THE AUTHOR

Inspired by her early love of Disney movies, Megan pursued a career in the feature animation industry and currently works as an animator in Los Angeles, California. In 2012, she started her MK Crochet/MK Knits pattern line, which has since been published and featured in various books and magazines.

Visit www.mkcrochet.com to learn more!

mk crochet ®

RESOURCES

Berroco
www.berroco.com
Comfort, Vintage, and Ultra Alpaca; available at local yarn shops and online.

Cascade
www.cascadeyarns.com
Sateen Worsted; available at local yarn shops and online.

Knit Picks
www.knitpicks.com
Wool of the Andes and Swish; available online.

American Felt and Craft
www.americanfeltandcraft.com
Online retailer of fine wool felts and noise maker inserts.